# A Cup of Comfort

## for *Sisters*

Stories tha
special bon

**ADAMS MEDIA**
Avon, Massachusetts

*For Linney and Nita—My sisters, my soul mates*

Published by
Adams Media, an F+W Publications Company
57 Littlefield Street, Avon, MA 02322. U.S.A.
*www.adamsmedia.com* and *www.cupofcomfort.com*

ISBN: 1-59337-097-0

Printed in Canada.
J  I  H  G  F  E  D  C  B  A

**Library of Congress Cataloging-in-Publication Data**
A cup of comfort for sisters / edited by Colleen Sell.
    p.        cm.
    ISBN 1-59337-097-0
    1. Sisters. I. Sell, Colleen.
    BF723.S43C86 2004
    306.875'4–dc22
                                          2004009499

This publication is designed to provide accurate and authoritative information with regard to the subject matter covered. It is sold with the understanding that the publisher is not engaged in rendering legal, accounting, or other professional advice. If legal advice or other expert assistance is required, the services of a competent professional person should be sought.

    —From a *Declaration of Principles* jointly adopted by a Committee of the American Bar Association and a Committee of Publishers and Associations

Many of the designations used by manufacturers and sellers to distinguish their products are claimed as trademarks. Where those designations appear in this book and Adams Media was aware of a trademark claim, the designations have been printed with initial capital letters.

*This book is available at quantity discounts for bulk purchases.*
*For information, call 1-800-872-5627.*

# Acknowledgments

At the top of my list of people to thank for their contributions to this book are the authors whose stories grace these pages. Their brilliant writing made it a success; their kindness made it a pleasure.

Vying for top billing on my gratitude list is the team at Adams Media, with the most valuable player award going to the *Cup of Comfort* "queen," Kate Epstein.

Were it not for my best friends and cheerleaders—my sisters Linney and Nita—I might never have pursued, much less realized, my dream of being a storyteller. They inspired my career; our sisterhood inspired this book.

I am equally grateful to the other members of my amazing family, especially my husband, Nikk, for putting up with the long hours I spend locked in my office, away from them, reading and compiling and editing each *Cup of Comfort*.

Most of all, I thank you, dear readers, for joining us in this celebration of sisters.

# Contents

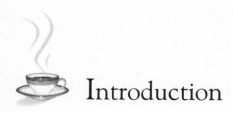 Introduction

"To have a loving relationship with a sister
is not simply to have a buddy or a confidante—
it is to have a soul mate for life."
—Victoria Secunda

I am the middle of three sisters, born in fast succession to our young Irish-American parents within a five-and-a-half-year span. As kids we could not have been more different: Nita, a.k.a. "Scooter," the oldest, a blond-haired, green-eyed jock turned prom queen, with a mean pitching arm and the voice of an angel; Linney, a.k.a. "Spider Monkey," the youngest, a tall, skinny, raven-haired, wide-eyed faerie princess turned rebel with a paintbrush, with a rich imagination and artistic talent to match; and me, a.k.a. "Buckwheat," the proverbial middle child, a shy, studious, dark-haired, dark-eyed nature girl turned cheerleader with a wild mane, wide smile, and stubborn steak. Despite our differing looks and personalities, the three of us "swell girls," as we called ourselves, also had a slew of things in common and got along well most of the time. But each of us has always danced to the beats of three very different drummers.

Today, in middle age, my sisters and I continue to celebrate both our commonalities and our differences. If anything, we've grown closer with time and fiercely protective and proud of those things that make us distinct from one another. Linney and Nita are my best friends not because we're related but because they are amazing women I genuinely admire, respect, and enjoy. And in sharp contrast to the "you-can't-have-the-same-parents" reaction we often received in our youth, we now look and sound almost identical. The "Irish triplets," our parents call us.

In the small Ohio town where we grew up and where we performed as a song-and-dance trio until my late teens (live that down in a small town), we are still, and apparently will forevermore be, known as "The Sell Sisters." When I returned to Kent for my twenty-fifth high school reunion (the only one I've attended), I was surprised by how many people asked about my two sisters. In fact, whenever my sisters or I speak to people from our hometown, they almost always ask about the other two sisters. It's as if the three of us are eternally linked in the memories and minds of those who knew us as the "Sell sisters."

Of course, those closest to us—our brothers and spouses and kids—know for a fact that we are linked—in, they say, some "weird, woo-woo, voodoo sisters way." Even my husband, Nikk, who joined my nutty family only eight years ago and is definitely not a woo-woo kind of guy, claims that there is an odd "vibe" between my sisters and me. The phone will ring, and having no forewarning of who might be calling, I'll say, "That's Linney" or "That's Nita" before picking up the phone, and it usually is. Or one of my sisters will e-mail about a dream or "feeling" they had about me, and it will mirror something that recently happened or subsequently happens. Or we'll independently send the same anniversary card to our parents or recommend the same book to one another or stub the same toe on the same night. And we can tell at a glance whether a new love is bad news or the perfect match for the gaga-blinded sister. I could fill an entire book with examples of our "sister voodoo." Then I could fill another book or two or three with the incredible experiences I've shared with my sisters. We are certainly not alone. Look inside any sister relationship and you'll find a wealth of interesting stories.

Not surprisingly, sisterhood has long been the subject of mythology, literature, and song. The Greeks even named a constellation after the myth of the seven sisters, the Pleiades. There is something otherworldly about the relationship between sisters, something fascinating and mysterious and spiritual that goes beyond flesh and blood and DNA and a shared history. I believe that the sisterly bond comes, like faith, from a deep knowing. A sister knows you in ways and at a level that no other person can—not your parents, your spouse, your children, not even your closest woman friends.

Only a sister knows that you screamed at your child for spilling grape juice all over the new carpet you scrimped and saved for. And only a sister then cleans up the mess, makes you chamomile tea, and puts you to bed for a nap while she takes your child to the park, because she also knows you need a break.

Only a sister knows that beneath the business suit of the smiling, composed, successful executive beats the heart of a bohemian longing to run bare-foot through a meadow of wildflowers and then capture them in watercolors on canvas, wearing your orange rock concert T-shirt and paint-splattered dungarees.

Only a sister knows that you hold your breath every time you cross a bridge, that your heart pounds from the rush of fight-or-flight adrenaline at the sight of a white pickup, that your stomach turns at the smell of cigar smoke. She knows why and never blows your cover. And she tries to protect you from these reminders of things you'd rather forget. And consoles you when she cannot.

Only a sister knows why you never expose your knees. And then buys you a miniskirt for your birthday and insists you look great in it. You don't believe her, of course, but she also knows that when the two of you go out for your birthday dinner, her treat, your lovely knees will turn heads. And they do. And you forgive her for telling you that your knees were "huge" that day in the sandbox when she was five and you were seven.

Only a sister knows about the "perfect love" who threw your love away. About your youthful embarrassment over your family's "less than" station in life and your conflicting feelings of pride and guilt when you rose above it. About the painful secret you kept even from yourself, until she blurted it out, not knowing you were not yet ready to face your own truth. And when you were, she reassured you it was okay, that you were okay, that you are perfect just as you are and worthy of the life and the love you have chosen.

Only a sister knows how you really felt when you stumbled and when you succeeded, when you fell from grace and when you were forsaken, when you reached your lowest valley and when you climbed your highest mountain.

Of all the blessings sisterhood can bestow, I think the greatest is to be known, really known. With deep knowing of another person comes understanding and acceptance and compassion and, ultimately, love.

My sisters know me. The essential me. The authentic me. The me I am when no one else is looking or listening, stripped bare of the labels and judgments and expectations and accoutrements of life. Just me. Buckwheat. The middle Sell Sister. Standing side by side with my bookends for life, Scooter and Spider Monkey. The two people I know better than anyone else on Earth.

In this beautiful collection of stories, you'll get to know many extraordinary sisters and get an intimate look at the magical bond that links them together, soul to soul. I hope their stories will entertain and comfort and inspire you, and I hope you will share them with all the sisters in your life.

—*Colleen Sell*

# Sister Power

"Mom . . ."
"Can we . . ."
"Have . . ."
"Ice cream . . ."
"Please?"

There they stood, five little girls, hair moist from the heat, proud of their newly discovered power to deliver single sentences in five sequential parts. How could I resist five sisters cooperating? They got ice cream. It was the first time they'd used their united strength to get what they wanted, but it wouldn't be the last.

When my daughters were teenagers, boyfriends were careful to be nice to all the sisters, not only to the one they wanted to date. If the sisters decided they didn't like a boy, the guy didn't stand a chance.

Phone calls were not forwarded and doors were not opened to the unwelcome.

One day I arrived home to find one of these poor suitors at our door, ringing the bell.

"I know they're in there," he said.

I opened the door, ushered him in, and sure enough, there they all were, drinking tea.

After he left I asked, "Why didn't you let him in? Where are your manners?"

"We don't like him."

"He's not good for her."

By the puzzled looks on their faces, they obviously thought I was the one who didn't get it.

One sister was so scared to bring her current boyfriend home that she met him away from the house for almost a year before he made it in.

College found the sisters in different schools but never farther apart than the telephone. When one needed consolation, she got it from four comforters; when one claimed a victory, the whole group celebrated. If one sister ran out of money and needed a place to stay between jobs or between schools, another opened her home until the crisis passed. They helped one another find jobs, and they lent and repaid loans to one another. Of course, they also fought and disagreed with each other, but they always stood united, ready to take on the next challenge, arm in arm.

Marriages and children did not ruin their collective front. The babies who came along year after year found not just Mom and Dad welcoming their arrival, but also four doting aunts and uncles with arms wide open. During one sister's labor, the hospital staff referred to the waiting room full of sisters as the "aunt trap." When nurses would pass by, one of the soon-to-be new aunts would intercept them and ask how things were going in the delivery room.

Babies were born to the first three sisters. Everyone was waiting for the fourth sister to make an announcement. She attended many baby showers with a smile on her face and an ache in her heart.

People outside the immediate family would smile and say, "You're next!" Or they would scold and say, "Don't wait too long. You're thirty; you can't wait forever."

They didn't seem to consider, maybe she can't get pregnant.

She didn't talk about the miscarriage at six weeks. Imagining the pain of mothers who lose a full-term baby or endure multiple miscarriages, she counted her blessings and kept trying. But the wait got longer and harder for her. Her husband researched all their options, and they picked a fertility clinic in the city where they lived.

For five years they tried to conceive a child, and each year their odds grew slimmer and their options fewer. Near Christmas of the fifth year, her younger sister gave birth to a healthy baby girl. Amidst the family's shared joy in the newborn's arrival, everyone, especially the new mom, felt the childless couple's sorrow.

With no baby to spoil, the childless couple doted on the nieces and nephews. So unselfish were they with their love for the new baby, it was hard to watch them go home with empty arms.

My four girls in Canada worried and talked about the toll it was taking on their sister in Atlanta. Her clothes hung too loosely, her cheeks were sunken, and the circles under her eyes were too dark for makeup to cover.

"It is time to give up. Accept. Adopt," I said. "Whatever it takes, but stop hurting like this."

Soon after Christmas, I got a phone call from one of the sisters.

"She is going to try a clinic in Toronto. They will work with the clinic in Atlanta and try some new procedures the facility in Georgia doesn't have. We are going to help."

Even though the treatments would involve thousands of miles of air travel and two fertility clinics, the sisters were determined. They had to try.

A pattern was established. Home base was a town near Toronto where four of the sisters lived. One sister stayed home to babysit and to fix meals for the travelers' families. The other three drove to the clinic in Toronto. One sister went into the operating room to hold her sister's hand. Afterward, pale and shaken from actually witnessing the pain of harvesting eggs or the invasiveness of that day's procedure, she reported the progress to the two sisters in the waiting room, where one sister knitted a blanket for the baby they all were sure would come.

Sometimes, the father was needed at the clinic. The sisters met his plane and embraced him, tried to ease his embarrassment, and afterward took him back to the airport immediately. With the mounting costs, missing work was not an option.

The first egg was implanted, and everyone held their breath. Three weeks later when it became clear a baby was not on the way, the sisters rallied around the couple, extending their support to the next procedure . . . and the next, however many and however long it took. The days following each procedure seemed unbearable. Each time a fertilized egg was implanted, the calls went back and forth between five sisters for three weeks, no one daring to ask the question on all their minds: What are the odds?

One time it was so close they felt certain her dreams were finally coming true. They were wrong. Another time, the doctors knew right away that the numbers were wrong and cancelled the day she arrived. Finally, after six months of treatments, the doctor told her, "It is not going to work. Your eggs are not viable."

The sisters mourned. They cried and prayed for another chance.

The whole family became so unnaturally quiet, it was scary. No one could relax. My computer hummed as I combed the Internet, researching adoption organizations. I knew the sisters, too, were searching for solutions.

Still, I had to sit down when I heard the voice of one of my daughters on the phone.

"Mom, there is one chance for her to have a baby: I'm going to donate an egg."

Now, two sisters would be caught up in the world of medicine and invasive procedures with no guarantee of success. Two families would have to cope with women on monthly doses of hormones that would rock their minds, upset their emotions, and distress their bodies. It took some time before I could support their decision. They didn't wait for me. The mighty force of five sisters was in full forward motion.

All sorts of good-luck routines became rituals: Leave for the city at an established time. Stop for chai tea at a certain place on the way. Keep exacting records of dates and times in a sacred, shared book. Light candles in a special room prepared for the travel-weary sister to recoup between procedures in the clinic so far away from her home.

The time between appointments was not easy. The donor sister took massive amounts of hormones; one month's medication filled a grocery sack. She wondered how her sister had been going through this and keeping her job as a substance abuse counselor. Some days, she cried all day. Others, she was lucky if she was able to sit and watch television. Coordinating a house full of kids with varying schedules was too much, so her sisters took turns caring for her children.

Four sisters learned how to give injections without fainting. They took turns driving. They cooked and cleaned for each other, so they could all keep their jobs. They worked together for six months, five families totally committed to helping each other get what one of them wanted.

At last, the tests were positive. The sudden inactivity was frightening. Every ringing phone was answered with fear. How could they stand it if it didn't work? Showers were planned; gifts were made with cold hands and worried hearts. Privately, I wondered whether the baby would be all right, whether, after all of this, the baby would be whole and healthy, whether she could carry it full term.

Finally, the twenty-eighth week, the date the doctor had said the baby would be reasonably safe, arrived. Everything looked fine. The sisters took a collective breath of relief.

Two drove and two flew to their sister's side when the doctor said it was time. He knew this was not a usual delivery when the father asked if all four sisters could be there. Generous nurses let the sisters give the water, wipe away the sweat, comfort, and encourage.

There they stood, four proud sisters surrounding the bed of one beloved sister, hair moist from the heat, eyes wet with tears.

"Mom . . ."

"We . . ."

"Have . . ."

"A . . ."

"Baby!"

—*P. Avice Carr*

# Blue, of Course

The first time my father made his famous blue pancakes, he misread the instructions and emptied an entire can of blueberries into the batter without draining the juice. That's how you get blue pancakes. Mom laughed and told him he should have used only the berries, but my sister, Janet, and I pleaded with Dad to continue making the pancakes his special way. I don't remember him ever turning us down.

One Sunday morning when Janet was four and I was five, Dad fixed blue pancakes as a way of coaxing Mom into the dining room. She'd been sick for several weeks fighting a nasty flu and couldn't seem to drag herself out of bed. Mom's doctor told her she was probably just extra tired from having two girls only a year apart, but that morning she was so weak she was having trouble talking. When the pancakes didn't draw Mom out of bed, Dad looked worried and starting pacing back and forth in the dining room. Finally, Dad left to see our neighbors, Mr. and Mrs. Swanson, because, besides being a good friend to our mom, Mrs. Swanson was also a nurse.

Janet and I knew something was wrong when the Swansons rang the doorbell a little later and asked both of us to accompany them to their house. Their faces told us this wasn't a time for questions, so we scrambled to put on our shoes, but before we could get out the door, an ambulance pulled into the driveway. Dad accompanied the two paramedics into the house, and we all silently watched as they calmly asked Mom questions. I remember thinking Mom probably didn't want us watching, but I was rooted to the floor and everyone seemed preoccupied. The paramedics consulted with each other, and after what seemed an agonizingly long time, they lifted Mom onto a stretcher and carried her out of the house. Even though Janet cried out, Mom barely moved.

Dad spoke a few words to the Swansons and rushed out to the waiting ambulance. The Swansons stayed with Janet and me, and after several restless hours, we learned Mom would be hospitalized with a syndrome that left her partially paralyzed and very weak.

Fortunately, it was August and Dad didn't need to be at work at the local high school for two more weeks. We all thought Mom would be back home by then, and though we were worried, we assumed everything would be fine. Then Mom took a turn for the worse. Dad told us as calmly as he could that because he was new to the school district, he had no vacation time and no emergency leave arrangements, and he didn't know what to do with his daughters. He sighed and admitted we might have to live somewhere else for a while.

Dad's sister, our aunt Evelyn, offered to help, but couldn't leave her job for more than a few days and had absolutely no experience with children. After lengthy discussions on the phone, Aunt Carmen, Mom's sister, said she would take Janet and me for as long as we needed. She lived in Cananea, Mexico, many miles from our central California home but was adamant that Janet and I would not go to foster homes, especially since we would have to be separated. Aunt Carmen had several children of her own and helped run their family business, but she convinced Dad that our being with her in Mexico was the best solution.

The Swansons drove Janet and me to Cananea on the same day Dad started his first day of classes. Dad told us there was no other option and that we were lucky the Swansons could drive us and that Aunt Carmen was willing to take us in.

When the four of us arrived in Cananea, we discovered that no one spoke English except our aunt.

The Swansons wanted to stay a while to make sure we would be all right but were reminded they had a long drive back. They gave Janet and me a warm embrace and told us to be brave for our mother. Right before they drove away, they handed each of us a new Raggedy Ann doll and told us to look in the dolls' pockets when we felt homesick. The Swansons departed, and Aunt Carmen had to leave for her office. All of a sudden, Janet and I realized we did not know anyone in the room and didn't understand a word anyone was saying. We tried not to cry, but it had been a long day and when Janet looked into her doll's pocket and pulled out a picture of our mother and father, we couldn't hold back the tears any longer. We felt so alone.

Aunt Carmen tried her best to look after us, but between her business and a busy household, she couldn't give us much attention. Because we didn't speak Spanish and didn't know the household routine, we simply tried to blend in. We were told no one knew whether our mother would survive or, if she did, whether she would be severely handicapped. Only time would tell.

As the weeks and months went by, we heard little news of our mother because there was so little progress to report. Janet and I began to learn Spanish and slowly grew accustomed to living in Mexico. Aunt Carmen was always distracted, but she was never unkind.

Janet and I shared a small bed, and right before we went to sleep each night, we'd take our pictures out of the dolls' pockets and put them beside the bed for the night. We always talked about going home. Sometimes we would cry, but mostly we were just sad that our mom was so sick. We could only hope that someday our parents would come for us.

After many months of hospitalization and rehabilitation, our mother did come back home, but she wasn't strong enough to raise children, so we continued living in Mexico for several more weeks. Finally, our dad called to say he couldn't stand the separation another day and announced that he and Mom were driving to Mexico to pick us up.

Suddenly, our wishes were granted, even though we had mixed emotions about leaving Mexico. By then, our Mexican family was important to us. After a restless night, Janet and I dressed in our best clothes and waited for our parents' arrival. Time seemed to stand still as the hours dragged by, then, in a blue flash, we saw our car. We still clearly remember Dad and a woman arriving in the driveway. We wondered who the lady was.

Aunt Carmen took us by the hand and told us the woman was our mother, but we didn't believe her. This small woman was encased in a metal brace from her waist to her neck. Her hair was short and dark, not long and blond like we remembered, and she was very frail, unlike the robust woman our mother was. Even her voice was different. She was definitely not our mother.

Then the woman explained that she had lost a lot of weight, had quit coloring her hair and had to wear it very short to keep it simpler to manage. But her high voice sounded very different, and when she reached for us, we both shrank from her.

Aunt Carmen and Dad comforted the distraught woman and angrily told my sister and me that we were making things worse. We were simply two little girls who wanted our mom back, but after upsetting everyone, we dared not say a word. After long farewells to our temporary Mexican family, we climbed into our car and left for California. During the lengthy ride, Dad explained that Mom's appearance had changed drastically but that she certainly was our mother. He said he worried that our young ages and the extended time we'd been separated might make it difficult for us to recognize this woman he insisted was our mom, but he was at a loss as to how to remedy the situation.

Janet took the picture of Mom and Dad out of Raggedy Ann's pocket and held it up to the woman. If you held the picture just right, there was some resemblance. Then Janet and I started asking questions: "Why is your voice different?" "Why are you so thin?"

The woman patiently explained how severe illness had taken a toll on her body and appearance, but even though the woman seemed familiar, Janet and I both still had our doubts. Janet asked more questions until finally she asked the woman what was the color of the pancakes we liked so much.

"Blue, of course," she replied. "Your father knows not to drain the blueberries when he fixes the pancakes for you two."

Janet reached over and patted the woman on the cheek and softly said, "Hi, Mom."

We knew then we were finally going home.

Unfortunately, Mom never regained her health, but she tried her hardest to raise us. Over the years, she was frequently ill. Every time we hit a snag and Mom got sick again, we always said the same three words. To this day when Janet or I have a problem, to put things into perspective and to assure each other that we can handle what life hands us, we say those three words only we two sisters understand: "Blue, of course."

—*Kathleen Brunson McNamara*

# Till Death Do Us Part

With the first snip I knew I had made a terrible mistake. If my sister Maureen was preparing to enter the life of a fourteenth-century monk or if she wanted to look like St. Francis of Assisi, then the haircut was well on its way to perfection. Considering she wanted to look like a seventh-grade Farrah Fawcett, the damage was beyond repair. Scissors in sweaty hand, I worked desperately, slicing random layers and angles into my younger sister's treasured mane. When I finally stopped long enough to breathe and admire my handiwork, I knew instantly that she'd never live down the horror just inflicted on her by her ninth-grade sister.

My only hope of salvaging this catastrophe, and saving my skin, was my gift of gab. Usually, I could talk myself out of anything and talk anyone, especially Maureen, into anything. Now, I needed to convince her that her new "do" looked just fine—great even. I'd have to rely on the same powers of persuasion that had swayed her to let me cut her hair in the first place.

For days, I'd pleaded with Maureen to let me "feather" her hair. "I can do it!" I proclaimed boldly. "You'll look great!"

Always the thinker, always the play-it-safe sister, she thought about it for what seemed like centuries before agreeing to let me take the orange-handled weapon to the hair she had spent thirteen years growing.

Her pondering drove me wild. Why think when you can act? That was my unspoken motto. My modus operandi was to jump on the sled and fly down the hill like a banshee, then deal with the stitches in the emergency room after knocking out the Stop sign with my forehead. My ever-cautious li'l sis, on the other hand, actually stopped to consider what would happen if she rode a sled with a broken steering column down a steep hill with a steel post planted at the bottom. She recognized the inherent danger of that joyride just like she knew that letting her amateur hairstylist sister have a whack at her hair was probably not a good idea.

You'd think that having a just-do-it older sister might have had something to do with Maureen's being the cautious creature she was, but she had been that way even as a toddler. Once, as we sat on the edge of the ironing board with a steamy iron nearby, I urged her to "touch it with one finger."

"C'mon, it's no big deal. Just do it."

"Mommy said no," she said matter-of-factly.

"Just touch it and see what happens," I coaxed. Couldn't she see the fun she was missing? The thrill of the risk? The allure of the danger?

It took several precious minutes to convince her that worlds of joy awaited her if only she would touch the darn thing before Mom got back. Her scream of pain did bring our mother back, in a flash, like a lightning bolt. And just as swiftly I was picked up, spanked, and returned to my seat before I knew what had hit me.

At the tender age of two and ever after, Maureen could be left in a room of outlets and forks, boiling pots, and matches and never risk harm to person, herself or anyone else, or property. She had an uncanny ability not only to learn things but also to apply them to life. I, on the other hand, was always looking for a new hot iron.

Several years after the iron incident, the two of us sat bored and idle in the stifling July heat that only a High Plains desert can produce. One of us decided it was a perfect day for a lemonade stand. Buoyed by the idea of making some quick cash, which was always in short supply, I jumped to my feet and dragged Maureen, whose motivation was no doubt to offer cool relief to our heat-oppressed neighbors, into the house. We scurried around mixing up a gallon pitcher of overly sweet honey water with a faint lemon flavor, grabbing a stack of Dixie cups from Mom's picnic supplies, and making a crude sign that read, "Lemonade: 10¢ A Cup."

All day we waited in the sun's heat, all the while sipping our own sticky tonic to cool off. It didn't take long to near the end of our supply—and without one customer passing our remote rural route that dead-ended nearby. We were close to calling the whole thing a bust when I heard the faint roar of an engine. Our expectations soared as we strained to listen to the approaching vehicle, peering over the hill leading to our small business on the verge of bankruptcy. We jumped up and down, waving our sign, and then the miraculous happened. The car stopped.

We leaned in the open passenger window. "Do you want lemonade?"

"Sure," the man replied.

We hastily filled the cup to the top with sun-warmed lemonade and thrust it in the window.

"Bring it to my side," he said. "I have the dime right here." He displayed the silver coin in his palm.

"Okay," I said and headed to the other side of the car.

"No, Marla." Maureen grabbed my arm as she backed away from the car.

Couldn't she see there was a dime for the taking? It would make this whole useless day worthwhile. Why was she holding me back? I broke free and started moving toward the man, who kept urging me forward.

"No, don't do it," Maureen said repeatedly.

Only her determined warnings made me hesitate. Suddenly, I felt afraid. I didn't know why I was afraid; I just knew I should be.

At that moment, one of our older sisters appeared, and the man sped off with his dime. If Maureen hadn't slowed me down, the rest of my life's history, if I would have had one, might have been rewritten.

It wasn't just danger that Maureen could sense. On the rare occasion that our sugar-fighting mother would allow us to have ice cream, I would swallow the icy crystals with super-hero reflexes. Maureen would sit quietly, lick her cone, pause to savor the taste, take another lick, pause to savor, and so on. As I'd come out of a brain-freeze that had thrown me on the ground in agony, I would watch her take one small taste and another, one after the other, slowly, reflectively, careful not to miss a drip. It had a hypnotic effect. The clock's ticking grew louder in my ears. My whole head seemed to be on fire. Only a taste of her ice cream could quench the flames of desire that had me prostrated before her.

"Maureen?" I'd say, as pathetically as possible. "Could I please have a really small lick of your ice cream?"

"No."

"Please," I'd beg, on my knees. "Just one teeny-tiny, itty-bitty, smallest-bite-ever-recorded-in-the-history-of-the-world?"

"No," she'd say adamantly. "Last time you promised to take only one tiny lick you took a really big bite."

Last time? What in the world did last time have to do with right now? Why didn't she just bring up the caste system in India for all it had to do with the present situation?

So, I would persist. "I promise on the Bible, on a stack of Bibles, I'll only take a little bite . . . Please, Maureen? . . . Just one small lick?"

Before long, she'd make a plea to my mother or father, who would intervene and demand I stop kissing my sister's shoes.

Although born less than fifteen months apart, our personalities were worlds apart. She pressed the clothes of her Sunshine family dolls. I cut off all my Barbie's hair and chewed most of their hands and feet. My clothes could be found on the floor or, if it was cleaning day, behind any piece of furniture; hers were always mysteriously hung up in the closet and neatly folded in drawers.

Yet, despite the fact that our brains operated on

two completely different frequencies, we were sisters through and through, with all that entailed. We shared marathon Barbie sessions, baby doll extravaganzas, hours of acting out self-scripted plays, late-night giggles, clothes, and the understanding that family was everything. We grew, we changed, we moved out, and we moved on with our individual lives.

As we made our separate ways in the world, we never really stopped to examine our influence or dependence on one another. Our relationship was comfortable, reliable, and totally uncontemplated.

One day when our two budding families were together, her husband, Scott, and I were engaged in our usual exchange of brilliance. He was teaching his small children to "moo" whenever they saw me, and I was trying to get them to say, "What's that smell?" every time he walked by.

My husband, Kevin, and Maureen watched us. They were used to Scott's and my banter, but that day, they were also comparing notes about how Scott and I did certain things the same way, about our similar annoying habits and quirks. Okay, so maybe Scott and I did have a few things in common—but, I suddenly realized, we certainly weren't alone.

Case in point: A few years earlier I returned home exhausted from a full day of undergraduate classes and a part-time job. I was looking forward to my date that night with Kevin, whom I had been seeing for only a few weeks. A girlfriend was with me when I came home and found the envelope on my apartment door. In it was a note from Kevin, explaining that the martial arts school where he studied was having a demonstration that night and at the last minute had asked him to help. He wrote that he'd love it if I could come, admission was five dollars, and he thought I might want to bring a friend. Also in the envelope were directions to the show and ten dollars.

My girlfriend's mouth dropped open. "You are so lucky!"

Kevin had thought the whole thing through. He understood that I was a broke student who didn't have five extra dollars, much less ten, and that girls prefer to travel in packs when going somewhere unfamiliar to see someone we don't know well. That day, that minute, I knew there was something about Kevin that I needed in my life—something familiar and very comforting.

I have five sisters, all of whom I could write long essays about. Each is amazing and loony in her own way. Each is essential to my life. But Maureen is different . . . she's the one I married.

—*Marla Kiley*

# Sisters of the San Joaquin

"Audrey," you said to me, "What are your most vivid memories of our childhood?"

"Roberta," I answered, though I called you Bobby when we were small, "I think my most vivid memory is actually one you've shared with me many times these seventy-some years."

Remember when I was a newborn and you sold me for a dime? Neighbors came to call and said to you, "That's sure a cute baby. Would you take a dime for her?" You took the dime and went and bought candy with it. When you came home, mother had moved the crib back into the bedroom. You thought the neighbors had taken me away and were seized with awful guilt. Struck with grief, you wailed, "Where's my baby sister?" Still, you ate the candy.

Remember when you scared "the shadow" out of the closet for me and swished the imaginary snake from under my bed with a stick?

You loved to tease me by pretending to be a bear. I'd say, "No. You are not a bear. You are my sister, Bobby!" But you'd continue to chant, "I'm Cubby Bear," and growl and walk around on all fours. I almost went out of my mind trying to get you to be my sister again. Part of me thought you really were Cubby Bear and I cried in frustration, but you wouldn't give in.

Remember when we climbed the ladders of wooden oil derricks? We wore white short-shorts and tied our blouses across our midriffs. We held the ladder rung with one hand and released a foot, arching our free leg in a coquettish pose.

We picked up horned toads with our bare hands. They made such intriguing pets, and we were reluctant to let them go. Sometimes we grabbed small lizards and were amazed when they separated from their tails and scurried into the sagebrush.

When I was sick, you sat on my bed and drew paper dolls. They looked like Ava Gardner, and you cut them out and drew outfits for every occasion, complete with tabs for holding the clothes to their shoulders.

Then one awful year you were sick with scarlet fever. With no penicillin then, the doctor had no choice but to simply monitor you through the crisis. When your fever raged, our parents doused you in a tub of cold water and your whole face swelled and your eardrums burst. Mother wept. Dad moved out of the house, because they had placed us under quarantine. I was told I must not go into your room, but I walked outside and crouched under your window. Not satisfied, I knocked on the pane until you heard me and sat up in bed. We mouthed words for a time with the glass between us, and then finally you lifted the window and I passed you the old doll we shared. Mother shook with anger and fear when she discovered us.

While you recuperated, everyone spoiled you rotten. Our parents bought you a new doll and burned the old one because it was contaminated. In the backyard, they threw your sheets and pajamas on the pyre. Then Dad moved back into the house from the bunkhouse where he'd been staying, and the county nurse removed the quarantine sign from the door.

"I'm going to town, Daughter," our father said. "What would you like Daddy to bring his little girl?" He was talking to you, and I was extremely jealous.

"I'd like some bobby pins," you said.

I burst into tears.

"Why are you crying?" Mother asked.

"If she gets Bobby pins, I want Audrey pins," I demanded.

Father laughed. Mother laughed. Our brother, Buddy, picked me up and whirled me around.

"Yes, you shall have Audrey pins," they said.

We begged for twin beds, fighting constantly for space in the big double we shared. Finally our parents made us a gift of a bedroom "suite," blond with a waterfall design. We were overjoyed and walked in and out of the bedroom all day, admiring it. That night I could not sleep. I missed you, my other spoon.

"Bobby," I hissed. "Bobby, can I sleep with you?"

"Why?" you answered sleepily.

"I'm scared."

You lifted the edge of your blanket and allowed me in your bed.

I betrayed you once. Your girlfriend Tiny asked me to steal your diary and give it to her. I was over-joyed to get the attention. While you were out of the house, I took your diary from your drawer. The next day on the bus, I opened my binder and took your most precious possession from where I'd hidden it overnight and put it in Tiny's hands. She read it aloud while you blushed crimson and the whole bus full of children, from six-year-olds to high school kids, roared with laughter.

"I'm in love with Duane Reichold." "Duane said 'hello' to me today." "Duane is the cutest boy in the world." "Mrs. Roberta Reichold," it said.

Do I have your forgiveness for that? If you'll grant

me absolution, I'll forgive you for selling me for a dime.

Even after that betrayal, you continued to protect me. You told me how babies are made. You made the way into high school safe, using your powers of persuasion to make sure I wasn't hazed as a freshman.

You remind me still of the glamour girls of the forties—Ava Gardner, Hedy Lamarr, Susan Hayward, Lana Turner. How come no one ever discovered you? When I look at you, I am once again in Lost Hills, climbing derricks, cutting out paper dolls, arguing over dishes, walking across the desert, riding the bus, looking at salt trees and gopher snakes.

You and I, Roberta, are sisters of the San Joaquin. We are toads and lizards and glamour queens and oil derricks. We are heat and poverty and hope and light. And because you are my sister and my very best friend, I have always known I am not alone.

—*Audrey Yanes*

# The Favor

It's hot—summer, humid, Maryland-in-late-July, sticky hot. My three sisters and I share a room, two to a bed, a jumbled mix of limbs and tossed sheets. All four of us hang over the mattress edges, trying to catch some semblance of a breeze from the small, round, putty-colored fan set smack in the middle of the room between the two beds. It barely manages to slice through the molasses-thick air.

I can't sleep. I feel unsettled from the heat, and my legs are jittery and jumpy, "growing pains" as Omi would say. I spot Barbara's foot on my side of the bed. We'd argued earlier, a disagreement of great importance, depth, and merit: She had played with *my* Barbie doll. So, I lean down and pinch up her sweaty big toe and move her foot over to her side. She doesn't even awaken, not a grunt out of her, but I am satisfied that the gross infringement is rectified. This is my right, of course—to punish her—because I am older, which is a right and a lesson handed down to me from my two older sisters, Sandi and Ann.

Ray, our only brother, is *the* oldest. He gets to sleep across the hall in the roomy, one-person-occupancy bedroom. He is leaving for Vietnam soon, and then it will be Ann's turn for the big room. I'm jealous, of course, but also maybe a little sad, not only because of Ray's departure from home but also because of Ann's departure from our shared room, although I would not, could not ever admit it. You see, I don't really mind sharing a room. We all fight, for sure, but less rather than more, and I like the activity.

I see Ann rise and head toward the bathroom. I watch her, spying. She turned sixteen in January, practically a grown-up, and she always bossed us around now, acting all moody or weird without rhyme or reason. The bathroom light casts a soft triangular glow into the bedroom. Highlighted in its light on the wall across from me I see the plaque, its shiny varnished finish casting a wet sheen in the heat. For a brief moment in my sleepy haze, I think the angel on the plaque is perspiring as well; she's working too hard to help the little girl across the bridge. Sometimes the picture scares me and I question it: Why only one child? Where are the rest of us? Where's Ray? Why is the angel helping only one girl, one sister, cross over? Where are Mom, Dad, Omi? Ann always reassures me that the others are already safely across, that this last little girl is crossing to meet everybody, that the beautiful angel has made sure all are safe.

Ann comes out of the bathroom, the light behind her silhouetting her shape. I see the glass of water shimmering in her hand as she walks over to Sandi. She dips two fingers in the glass and slowly flicks droplets of water, showering them across Sandi's face, then her upper body, then her lower body, and then, last, she dips four or five times into the glass, letting each rivulet fall puddlelike onto Sandi's pillow.

Ann moves to me next. I keep my eyes closed, letting the water bless my body. It feels cool and refreshing. The jitteriness in my legs begins to calm, and the heat momentarily dissipates. For the first time that night, I feel the wind from the fan sail across my body like a lilting, elusive breeze, escorting me to sleep.

Barbara is last. Like Sandi, she doesn't wake. Like me, she doesn't stir. And all of us sleep more peacefully.

Now, thirty years later, I stare down at Ann, the small hospital bed made larger by her thinned body. The bed is a necessary intrusion, a bulky, clumsy invader. Her real bed is pushed to the side. We—Sandi, Barbara, and I—take turns trying to sleep there, the bedspread and sheets in a continuous rumple.

We use wet towels to cool her down. Her temperature remains dangerously high, her body so hot it is surely boiling her blood. Sandi goes into the adjacent bathroom to fill the syringe with the Adavan and morphine cocktail. The light from the bathroom filters out across Ann's bed and halos her head.

The seizures started two days ago, making Ann's arms and legs flail about. We can do nothing to stop them, nothing to stop the painful dance of cancer eating away at her body, but we try. Barbara kneels at the foot of the bed rubbing Ann's feet, while Sandi and I gently hold her arms that kink rigid from the spasms. We hear the bones snap from the poison that has spread to her marrow. We whisper to her, sharing stories from our childhood, offering prayers of peace and calm, but nothing seems to work, for cancer knows no religion or peace. Ann, always the boss, always the organizer, has already told us her wishes, down to picking out her own tombstone and the songs she wants sung at the funeral.

I see the old plaque from our childhood bedroom hanging on her wall above her bed. I realize with a pang that the child in the picture is Ann, that she is moving across the bridge from earth to heaven and that we are not waiting on the other side for her, but she will be waiting up there for us. I hope the angel helps her across. Surely her God will ease her pain and suffering soon. I cannot fathom the reason why

Ann, so devout and so trusting of God's will, must suffer so, and I have long stopped waiting for an answer. While her deep faith has helped her through this, her suffering has accelerated the abandonment of mine.

At the sink, I dampen more washcloths. With one, I will wash her face; her teeth have bit down again onto her lips, causing them to bleed. As I re-enter the bedroom, Sandi and Barbara look up at me and reach out for a cloth. We cool her papery skin with the damp cloths, grateful to return the favor from so long ago, hoping with silent prayers that it is enough, wishing her a peaceful sleep before her walk across the bridge.

—*Rebecca C. Christensen*

# When Lightning Strikes

"*Sister for Sale: 50¢*," the sign around my neck reads—placed there by my two older sisters, who reassure me with doe eyes and honey-dipped voices, "*You'll see . . . things will be better this way.*" They watch from the bushes as I stand alone on the side of the road like a used car. After several minutes pass with no takers, my older sister returns, scowling, and with a black crayon marks me down to 25 cents. She darts back to my other sister, and snickering, they high-five. With cold reality followed by a hot rush of anger, I'm on to them: They just want to get rid of me.

At that point in the dream, which recurred throughout my childhood, I always woke up.

Though my two older sisters never actually tried to sell me, I'm sure they would have liked to, so my nightmare had more than just a toehold in reality. I guess you could say there was tension between us as kids. I, of course, was always the innocent victim of their heartless shenanigans . . . well, almost always. This wasn't your average sibling rivalry. But then, ours was not exactly an average American household.

You see, our parents split up when we were very young and at a time when divorce was rare, and we lived with our dad, which was also rare then. That put Molly, the oldest at eleven, in the tight spot of having a great deal of responsibility when she was still just a kid. It made Molly and ten-year-old Rachel "best friends." And it put me, age seven and the odd sister out, at the mercy of Molly and Rachel's united front.

Of course, Molly and Rachel fought sometimes, too, but mostly they operated as a team against a common enemy: me. Not that I did anything to deserve it, being that I was the nice one of the lot.

Because she was the baby of the family and, some said, soooo cute, Anna got off easy. Nobody dared pick on her. Actually, it never occurred to me to pick on Anna. Maybe, having suffered the slings and arrows of the dastardly duo all my young life, I took pity on Anna and so spared her the aggravation. So, you see, I really was the nice one.

When I did lob a spike at Molly or Rachel, it was always deserved, in retaliation or self-defense. And I never deliberately annoyed them—except for a few times. And I didn't actually enjoy provoking them— much. And since they had the upper hand, considering the differences in our ages and that there were two of them against one of me, I had to be creative with my revenge.

Take, for example, the Ice Cream Incident—a stroke of genius that Molly and Rachel now use as proof that I did, indeed, deserve what I got.

Every Sunday afternoon, Dad would pile us in the car and take us out for ice cream cones. Anna sat in front next to Dad. We three older girls sat in back. In those days, back seats had a hard hump in the middle. So, of course, that's where I had to sit, flanked on either side by my sworn enemies, Molly and Rachel, who, by virtue of seniority and always calling "dibs," got the window seats.

Every week, the same routine repeated itself.

"Here's your ice cream, girls," Dad would say cheerily.

"Thank you, Daddy," we'd coo.

Within minutes, my big sisters would gobble down their ice cream, cones and all. Only when they were finished and licking their fingers did they pause to look around. That's when they'd notice me, slightly elevated like a queen on the bump between them, with almost all my ice cream left.

Now, I had something they wanted, and I figured they were feeling pretty sorry they'd been mean to me. But with Dad close by, I knew they couldn't exactly tie me up and swipe my cone. So, I'd take a long, slow lick and look at Molly. Then a long, slow lick and look at Rachel. Then another lick and look at Molly, then another lick and look at Rachel, back and forth, while they glared at me in furious silence until they could take it no more.

"Daddy!" they'd wail in unison. "Teresa's bugging us!"

"What's she doing?"

"She's looking at us!"

"Oh, for crying out loud," Dad would moan, pulling the car over so he could referee.

Swiveling around, he'd see me sitting still, eyes straight ahead, one hand around my cone, the other holding a napkin in my lap, minding my own business, innocently eating my ice cream.

"Want some, Daddy?" I'd ask, holding my ice cream out to him, proving I was a good sharer.

"You two stop picking on your sister!" he'd holler.

Then would come my moment of crowning glory.

"Teresa, come up here and sit in the front with me and Anna, so your sisters can't bother you."

"Okay, Daddy," I'd say dutifully, handing him my cone to hold while I climbed over the seat. If I accidentally kicked Molly or Rachel on the way over, well, that was just a bonus.

The whole way home, I didn't dare glance back at them, for fear their looks might actually kill me.

Decades later, Molly and Rachel still claim I

deliberately subjected them to Torture by Ice Cream. Really, I was just a delicate eater, being oh so careful not to dribble ice cream on my chin or on Daddy's car. I was so misunderstood back then.

Another childhood story Molly and Rachel like to trot out as evidence that they had every right to pummel and harangue me is The Disappearing Allowance Incident—though I don't remember any of it and swear they're making it up.

Every Friday, Dad would give us each a dollar, no small sum in those days, and take us to a five-and-dime to spend it. Molly and Rachel would blow every penny on various dime-store treasures, while I, the eternal spendthrift, would buy a small treasure or two, never using my whole dollar and stashing the change in a secret hiding place. Slowly, my coin cache would swell to a fistful of nickels and dimes, which, of course, I planned to put to some noble use, such as feeding orphans.

Every so often, like clockwork, Molly or Rachel would lament they had no allowance left to buy a candy bar or a Coke or the newest teenybopper magazine. Sadly, this is where their story again twists and borders on slander. According to Molly and Rachel, I'd dash off to my bedroom and come back with a closed fist, prance around the room in front of them, and then stop suddenly and open my hand to reveal my secret stash of coins, which, coincidentally, added up to more than enough to buy whatever they were yearning for.

"Teresa, can we borrow some of that?" they'd ask in their fake sweetest voices. "We'll pay you back. Really."

That's when I'd laugh fiendishly and hurry off to hide my money again—according to my sisters. Truly, I do not remember this, and frankly, their assertion that I was a selfish money hoarder just doesn't add up: I get paid a lot more than a dollar a week now, and I never have so much as a fistful of nickels left over to stash away.

The one act of revenge to which I do lay claim is a stroke of vengeful genius I call The Chicken Potpie Caper of 1963.

One night for dinner Dad baked a bunch of frozen chicken potpies. There were few meals I despised more than chicken potpie. Molly and Rachel didn't seem to mind, and Anna ate whatever she was given.

After Dad finished his dinner, he got up and lifted a sleepy Anna out of her high chair.

"I'm going to put the baby to bed," he said. "You three girls don't leave the table until your plates are clean."

Soon, Molly and Rachel finished their pies and ran off to play, leaving their empty plates on the table. Meanwhile, I struggled on the horns of a dilemma. It was almost time for *My Three Sons* to come on television and I hadn't eaten a bite of my pie. I couldn't leave the table with the loathsome thing still on my plate, so I did what I had to do. I finished just as my show's theme song began.

Ten minutes later Dad bellowed, "Molly! Rachel! Get in here!"

"Yes, Daddy?" they said in unison, rushing to the kitchen.

"Didn't I tell you to finish your dinners before you left the table?" he asked, pointing to the table. There, on each of their plates, sat the damning evidence: half a chicken pie. My plate was sparkling clean.

"But . . . ," said Molly.

"But . . . ," said Rachel.

"No buts! What kind of example are you girls setting for your little sister? Don't you know she looks up to you two?"

Meanwhile, I remained glued to the TV. I could almost feel the white-hot heat of four angry eyes burning holes through my pigtailed head—especially when Dad came into the living room to watch TV with me. I was dying to sneak down the hall and find out just how mad Molly and Rachel were at me, but I stayed put in Dad's lap.

I don't remember what their punishment was, nor do I recall them avenging my little trick. But I'm pretty sure that's when the sister-for-sale nightmares started.

I wish I could say that these were merely isolated icebergs on a warm sea of sisterly love. But such bickering and battles permeated all of our growing-up years. Finally, during our late teens and early twenties, we struck an unspoken truce, and the common experiences that had polarized us began to connect us. The lightning storm that had torn apart our family—the sudden and final end of our parents' marriage—eventually became the shared history that brought us closer.

Together, my sisters and I form a four-person support network. When one falters, the others rush in to hold her up. As adults, we've shared triumphs as well as trials and truly enjoy spending time together. When I was a kid, if you'd told me I'd one day say my sisters were nice people I could trust and relate to, I'd have stuck half a chicken potpie on your plate. But it's true.

While I'm at it, I might as well come clean on a few other things: I wasn't a totally innocent victim in our childhood skirmishes. Anna really was as cute and sweet as everyone said. Molly and Rachel weren't the mutant offspring of the evil flying monkeys of *Wizard of Oz* fame I accused them of being. In fact, all three of my sisters are intelligent, creative, compassionate, fun-loving, nice people.

But I'm still the nicest.

—*Teresa Ambord*

# My Sister, the Mother

It was late afternoon, I remember, and Ethan was home from his first round of chemo, a day or so before he would be a full six months old. It was after the tears had stopped—after the piercing diagnosis, the slur of first days, the nights that had crackled with terror—and I had spent the day with my sister, playing at normality, working harder than we'd ever had to work at make-believe. I had just finished buttoning my coat, had turned back toward the kitchen to say goodbye, and there she was, my sister—who paled and looked away whenever a doctor pricked her finger—placing a syringe in her baby's "central line" to force back the blood that had started to seep. My sister, the mother, I thought, and those words still caption my memory of that moment.

My memories of moments not long before that one are like snapshots filled with color and light: My sister, standing sideways, her head back in laughter, her swollen middle silhouetted against the hues of July. Ethan, in the delivery room, swaddled in powder blue, raising a fist in salute to the father he'd just met. The three of them, where there had been two: Ethan nestled in my sister's arms, her husband leaning in for a closer look—realizing they'd just reinvented the world. And my sister again, weaving the buggy through Michigan Avenue's crowds—a balloon tied to its handle, Ethan's booties kicking in the air, the giraffes and zebras on the mobile above him dancing and whirling. I'd been standing across the street that morning when I'd looked up and suddenly seen them, and I remember thinking that they were a parade unto themselves.

But then—overnight—the snapshots changed to black and white.

In one, Ethan's parents, grandparents, and I are gathered in a circle around him, on the day when he awoke with one of his eyes protruding. "It's an infection," we told ourselves, or, "He's bumped himself on a toy." "Look how he's smiling and cooing and playing," we said—and said again, too loud, too urgent—"and eating; he's eating so well." "The doctor will laugh at us for worrying," we laughed—to prove that it was true—as we zipped him into his bunting and tied his hat beneath his chin. By that night he was sleeping in a crib in the Four West wing of Children's Memorial.

When my sister and I were growing up—less than two years and rarely more than three feet apart—we tried on motherhood every time we draped ourselves in our dress-up clothes. But nowhere we had ever imagined pushing our babies in our high-heeled wanderings had prepared us for the realities that awaited us in Four West. A mere elevator ride away from the state of denial the lucky inhabit—where it's possible to believe that bad things happen only to other, faceless people—Four West is a place where the unthinkable is routine and what was once routine is no longer thinkable. Where every door opens to reveal a family frozen in flight, battling gravity. Where children ride on the bases of IV poles down the halls instead of on bicycles down the street, their teddy bears swinging from the hooks above them, their every giggle and wave and shout a more defiant thumb in death's eye than no-handed wheelies could ever be. And adults leave it to their glances to speak the words their lips will not.

The images within my memories of my first visit there are tilted at drunken angles, as though my internal camera was jarred each time it clicked. From within the pea-green haze that envelops what I remember of that day emerge slanted walls and crooked doorways, floors that slope and windows that list, lights that spew a neon snarl of jagged edges. There is one image, though, that is more discernible than the others. It is of the three of them again, Ethan and his parents, clustered by his crib— deportees from the state of denial, looking lost. That image lingers as an ache every time I recall it.

Early in my life, before I was certain of much else, I was certain that I was to be my sister's protector— that, although I was the younger, the quieter, the less outgoing, and although she was gifted with bright- ness and beauty, she was more vulnerable than I to the blows of a bruising world. There I am at three, in the album of family remembrances, hurling myself headlong into the belly of the six-year-old bully who'd punched her. And at five, marching up to the teacher who'd forgotten to give her her skating race ribbon. "That," I am announcing, thrusting an indig- nant mitten, "belongs to *my sister*." And at ten, out- side her cabin during our first stay at overnight camp, shrinking from the Minnesota darkness and the cries of distant loons, waiting for her to answer my knock and lean out the window—so I can whisper good- night to her. It was the closest I could come to tucking her in.

On that first day in Four West, I began to under- stand that the darkest night we'd ever known had fallen and I couldn't tuck her in. Every time a nurse took Ethan from my sister's arms and carried him off—for blood tests and blood typing, for a bone scan and a CT scan, for an MRI, an X-ray, a bone marrow aspirate—I wanted to snatch him back and hiss, "He belongs to *my sister*." But instead, I had to watch him go and to watch her watch him go, and when he would finally reappear, he would be limp and sedated and pale. Those days assaulted like a siren keening.

Then, in the next days, after Ethan went home for the short time before treatment, the instant of numbness that follows a breath-sucking impact evaporated, leaving his family rocking in pain. In every memory I gathered of my sister then, she is weeping. The night before Ethan's return to the hospital, I found her crumpled in the bathroom, sobbing, "I can't do this. I can't go through this. I'm just so scared." And instantly, I envisioned a moment we'd lived years before, during the summer when I was six and she was eight, when she climbed the ladder of the highest diving board at the city pool, inched her way to the edge of the swaying plank—and froze. Thirty feet below, I felt her terror. "You don't have to do this," I screamed up to her, not caring who heard. In the end, my sister inched her way back to the steps and climbed down to solid ground.

This time, as Ethan's mother, she leapt.

When she surfaced, back in Four West, the world as she had known it had been replaced by another, and I saw homesickness in her eyes. When I think of her then, it's as though she were groping her way through this alien landscape, where "bed" was a chair next to Ethan's crib. Where dinner was gulped, standing, between crises and cries. Where people who'd known her all her life weren't certain what to say to her and those she'd met just moments before—those whose children lay nearby—could speak with her as though they'd known her all her life.

I can see her standing by the window of Room 486 late on that first morning, knowing that her baby, whom she'd always protected—from startling noises and glaring lights and icy gusts of wind, from smoky rooms and jutting corners and bee stings and germs, from strangers and from pain, from sadness—was now lying inert on an operating table with steel slicing his skin to insert a "central line" through which toxic substances would flow. In that snapshot, I see her recognizing that, in this world where she now resided, she was expected to view such brutality as protection. On her face, that recognition looks like the imprint of a slap.

But then, there she is, later that day, bent over the tubes sprouting from a plastic torso, learning to inject and draw, to flush and swab, to clamp. And there she is the next morning, *mooing* and *oinking* to the tune of "Old Macdonald"—verse after verse, until Ethan laughs, another verse, then another, until he squeals—while chemotherapy drips into his veins. And there she is, masked and gloved, holding him still, despite his wails, while a nurse changes the dressing covering his surgical wounds. And there, sweeping the sheets of his crib, gathering clumps of the hair he'd just grown, and then talking to the doctors in a language still foreign to her. *Carboplatin*, she is saying, and *neutropenic*. *Growth colony stimulating factor* and *hyperalimentation*. *Nasogastric tube* and *absolute neutrophil count*. *Anti-emetic*. And that's my sister, too, her back and shoulders steeled, her eyes sending flashes of warning, telling the resident who's predicted this treatment's failure that if he wants to practice doom-and-gloom medicine, he can find somewhere else to do it, because this baby, her baby—Ethan—is going to recover.

I remember that, toward the end of the last day of that first round of chemo, at just about the time when Ethan would have been playing on the kitchen floor, with twilight pressing against the windows and soft jazz drifting through the room, when he would have been watching his parents shed the workday and settle into the evening—chatting with each other, preparing for his bath, putting pasta to boil on the stove—when he would have been waiting for that moment when his father would scoop him up and toss him in the air and his mother would pretend he was a jet plane, dipping and soaring to the changing table, a nurse came in to say he needed one more test. For an instant, I saw my sister flinch and her eyes begin to fill, but then, pushing her headband firmly back on her hair, she stood up. And they started slowly down the hall, a parade unto themselves.

In that snapshot, Ethan is peering over his father's shoulder, trailing a jumble of wires and tubes. The nurse is behind them, pushing the IV pole. And a few feet back, bringing up the rear, with a pacifier in one hand and an emesis basin in the other, with a Barney doll stuck in her pocket and a tube clamp hanging from her belt, with her eyes a shade too bright, but a determined tilt to her chin, is my sister—making faces at Ethan until he squeals.

—*Laura S. Distelheim*

A version of this story was published in *Whetstone*, Volume 13, 1996.

# Love Through Nine Bananas

On my whatnot shelves between the cups and saucers from my grandmother stands a small assortment of unique people. These figurines—otherwise known as the "Banana family"— were all carved from a block of redwood, one by one, over a period of eighteen years, by my sister Barb, a gifted artist. The first one, Banana Jane, was carved thirteen years after her inception, the product of our young imaginations during a long, hot automobile trip to the Grand Canyon.

Barb and I shared the front seat with our father, the sole driver on such vacations. Our big station wagon had no air conditioning, and the wind, by turns fresh and stifling, whipped through the open windows, tangling our hair and salting our sweaty foreheads with fine grit. As the miles slipped by and with hours of driving still ahead, my mind began to wander, conjuring up a story to occupy the time.

"I could tell you about Banana Jane," I said out loud, having no clue where the story might go.

"What? Who?" Barb asked.

"Banana Jane," I repeated, as if her name were a common household word. "Um, she's a banana inspector . . . and she lives and works in the jungles of Bengor."

"Bengor? Where's that?" Barb began to enter into the spirit of the story.

"Africa," I said.

At that point, Barb caught on to the game, and together we spun our tale as we zipped down the highway through Kansas and Nebraska. In the backseat, our mother and younger sister grew quiet, listening intently to the excellent adventures of Banana Jane.

Though Jane's responsibilities as a banana inspector were, and remain, a bit vague, her image and personality emerged crystal clear. Jane was a highly intelligent, scientifically minded young lady. Her work attire consisted of Army-green shorts and a camp shirt, with matching pith helmet and kneesocks. Sensible shoes protected her feet from the dangers of the tropics, and a pair of binoculars hung perpetually around her neck. Quiet and mild-mannered, Jane was absolutely geeky in a pleasant kind of way.

Near the Colorado border, Barb's notebook and pencils came out. As I continued to narrate the story, she made notes and drew pictures, bringing our imaginings to life. A suitor came into Jane's life, a fellow inspector by the humble name of Chuck Champion. The quintessential nerdy genius, Banana Chuck sported a flattop haircut and a slight paunch under the "Bananas Forever" logo emblazoned on his T-shirt. Kneesocks and sensible shoes completed his ensemble, and he carried his banana manual and mechanical pencil everywhere. If personal computers had existed in 1968, Chuck would have carried a laptop. With Jane, he was always a gentleman, never forcing his affections on her, perfectly content with holding pinky fingers for twenty years.

Jane came by her fascination with bananas quite naturally: Her father, General Top Banana, had worked in the plantations for years. The General bore a striking resemblance to Teddy Roosevelt, with a silver handlebar mustache and wire-rimmed spectacles. Acutely aware of the dangers of the jungle, he kept a revolver strapped to his side. Jodhpurs and bush jacket formed his jungle wear, along with— yes—the requisite kneesocks and sensible shoes.

On southward through the spectacular Rockies we drove—and the Banana family grew.

Jane's mother, Hannah Banana, had a penchant for making banana bread. Clad in a long blue dress and striped apron with her white hair twisted into a graceful bun, she was quite the proper lady. Whether she wore kneesocks or thick support stockings under her skirt we couldn't decide and probably will never know, but she surely wore sensible shoes. To my delight, we rode the mules down into the Grand Canyon that summer, an adventure I still talk about today. At the campground we struck up a friendship with a Swiss family with whom my parents still exchange Christmas cards. The Grand Canyon trip deepened our appreciation for the marvelous country we live in and whetted our appetites for exploring more of it. Additional journeys followed in subsequent summers, and new adventures of Banana Jane & Company unfurled with each vacation, always illustrated with Barb's drawings.

As we grew older, the Banana family languished but never completely died. We put away the pictures when we got home after each vacation, but never threw them out. Every now and then, a conversation would jog a memory. "Just like Banana Jane and Chuck," Barb would say to me, and off we would go again, laughing and embellishing the stories a little more ornately.

While the Banana family remains ageless, we do not. Barb and I grew up. I married and moved hundreds of miles away. Though my new roommate was wonderful, I missed my old one, Barb, with whom I had shared a room for nineteen years. Those first six months of marriage were the longest and loneliest of my life.

"Shall we go home for Christmas?" asked my kind husband, knowing my answer even before he asked.

Amidst the bounty under my parents' twinkling Christmas tree that year was a small package for me from my sister. The wrappings came away to reveal a small wooden figure standing demurely inside her little box. The inscription on her base read, "To Jackie from Barb: Banana Jane, born 1968." Over the next fifteen years, Jane traveled with me from home to home, always taking up her place next to Grandmother's cups. Eventually Chuck came to join her, and then the General and finally Hannah moved onto the shelves.

During a summer reunion at a cabin on a wooded lake, Barb and I decided that, since we had created the Banana family, their future was in our hands: We could complete the stories even though we were all grown up. Thus, after a decorous twenty-year courtship, Chuck and Jane got married. Five children came to bless their union, all brought to life with my sister's carving knife: son Dole, slim and athletic; daughters Chiquita (who hugs a little doll, Frondie, tightly to her chest) and Peele; and a tiny basket cradling twins nicknamed "Banana Split." None of the children wears socks or shoes.

As the years went by, Barb and I continued to be

close, talking on the phone frequently and visiting back and forth. Then came a falling out that put a strain on our relationship, and we became distant. Though my heart ached at the almost hostile gulf between us, I could not see a way to bridge it. I wasn't even completely sure of what had caused the rift. In time, however, as I cooled off and stepped down off my high horse of self-righteousness, I saw my part in the problem. So I wrote Barb a letter, asking her forgiveness. To this day, I don't recall whether she ever responded to my letter, or to any of my letters, as I wrote several, apologizing and trying to mend things between us. Little by little, she has thawed toward me, and we are working our way back to one another and toward a better relationship than ever before.

In the course of moving from Florida to Colorado to Ohio to Pennsylvania, Banana Jane has changed very little. Her pith helmet is slightly chipped in front, and the hot African sun has tanned her redwood skin. But she retains her girlish figure and placid expression, as she stands contentedly with her family on my whatnot shelves, reminding me always of the love between two sisters.

—*Jacquelyn A. Kuehn*

# The Green Coat

My sister, Norma, has always been a hard worker, earning the title "my big girl" from our mother, while I was always labeled "lazy Joan." Norma deserved her title. I'm not too sure I deserved mine. Norma went to work when she was barely twelve years old, doing weekly cleaning for an elderly neighbor lady. The following year she went to work taking care of a frail lady who had breast cancer.

Even though Mrs. Harding was very sick, she ran a boarding house from her bed, giving Norma directions on how to prepare the evening meal and do the laundry for the men who rented rooms upstairs. The house was one of those turn-of-the-century shotgun houses that gave a clear view from front to back, and from her bed Mrs. Harding could see Norma as she did her chores.

The men came in from work at night and hungrily ate the beans and cornbread or boiled potatoes with cubes of meat that had simmered in rich broth all day. Norma didn't keep the money she earned. It went directly to Mother to help with the household expenses. Even though Dad was working a good job at that time, things were still a bit tight.

After Mrs. Harding died, Norma immediately got a job as a soda jerk at a drugstore. She worked on the far north side of town, and we lived on the far west side. I would sometimes ride a bus out to the drugstore and sip Cokes while she worked. I'd wait around until she got off work and ride the bus home with her.

I started high school in September 1946. Norma and I walked to school together each morning. We even sat next to one another in the same homeroom. When the final bell rang for the day, Norma would go racing out to catch the early bus to make it to work on time while I leisurely dawdled in the hallway with new friends. I usually ended up down the street at a little hamburger place, sipping cherry-flavored Cokes and learning to smoke Lucky Strikes.

The forty-five-minute walk to school soon became less fun as October brought fall rains and cold air down from the north. Mother kept telling me to put on my winter coat. The coat from the previous winter when I was still in grade school was ugly brown tweed with a darker brown velvet collar. The sleeves were too short, and since I had grown through the summer months, the waist of the coat was nearly under my armpits.

Norma and I were just twenty-two months apart in age and had finally reached equal size, so there were no hand-me-down clothes. Actually, Norma was having the same problem I was, with her coat being too small.

Mother kept telling me that she didn't have the money for a new coat, and I kept refusing to wear the little girl's coat to school. I stomped, I pouted, I begged. It didn't do any good. After several punishments, I finally put on the old ugly tweed coat and started out to school. Once I was out of mother's view, I took it off and put it around my shoulders. Some of my classmates were donning their new coats with the fashionable short A-line style. How I envied those girls.

By early November the snow had started to fall, the north wind swirling it around my bare head as I walked to and from school. Mother was already planning our annual family Thanksgiving dinner. She had just gone over the guest list and menu with me when I made the mistake of asking her the wrong question.

"How is it that you can buy all those groceries to feed everyone but not buy me a new winter coat?"

"Young lady, it isn't always about you and what you think you need," Mother scolded and promptly sent me to my room for my selfish attitude.

Norma came home from work at eleven o'clock that evening. I could hear her voice full of enthusiasm in the room below me. Our upstairs bedroom had open registers in the floor to allow the warm air from the downstairs heating stove to warm the room. I bent down and pressed my ear against the register. I could see Norma moving about. I gasped. She had on a beautiful new coat. Hot tears stung my eyes.

Just then Mother called to me, "Come down and see what Norma has bought with her paycheck."

I wiped away the envy tears and descended the stairs. Norma twirled round and round, showing off her new coat. Then she ran into Mother's bedroom and returned with a big box and handed it to me. Wordlessly, I dropped to my knees, opened the box, and started pulling aside the tissue paper.

Inside was the most beautiful coat I had ever seen: the new short A-line style with an attached hood, in a gorgeous leaf green. I looked up into my sister's face. Tears of joy glistened in her eyes as a wide grin covered nearly her whole face. I held the coat close, brushing it gently with my hands, and even though it was against my nature to cry in front of anyone, I could not fight back the lump in my throat that caused tears to trickle down my cheeks.

As I slipped my arms into the sleeves of my new coat, Norma chattered about how she'd been saving her money since school started to buy a new coat.

"But I couldn't put on a new coat knowing you needed one too, so I had to wait until I had enough money for two coats," she explained.

I've had many new coats since then but none as special as the green coat my big sister bought for me when I was thirteen. Over the years, my sister and I have shared many special times and exchanged many special gifts. To this day, Norma never visits empty-handed, nor do I allow her to leave without tucking something special under her arm. But the greatest gift has always been that we are sisters.

—Joan Watt

 Houses of Gold

I was eight and my sister, Gertie, was six the day we first saw the hundred-year-old house on Exchange Street. The late-afternoon sun slanted through the entry-hall window and glowed on the gilded walls. I drew my fingers across the shiny smoothness.

"Don't touch," said my mother, brushing away my hand. She frowned at Gertie, whose fingers were poised to imitate mine.

That summer, my father had been made plant manager of the local gypsum mine. Number 5 Exchange Street, only a few blocks from our old neighborhood, belonged to a different world. Gold-brushed leather, hand-painted with grapevines and bunches of bluish-purple grapes, covered the dining room walls. With its slate roof, two fireplaces, and three covered porches, it was the finest house in the village of Akron, New York.

Gertie and I sat on the entry-hall floor, our box of crayons between us. Outside, rain drizzled down. Mom had gone shopping.

"See, Gertie?" I said as I outlined gold-petaled flowers with red. I wasn't touching the wall with my fingers, just the crayon. Mom was going to like our decorations.

My sister picked out a blue crayon and started drawing a puppy. I thought a butterfly would look nice on top of the flower. I'd just added whiskers to a golden cat when I heard Mom open and close the back door.

"Let's surprise her," I whispered to Gertie.

She nodded and followed me into the kitchen.

"It's almost dinnertime," Mom said. "I want you girls to wash and snap those green beans."

Mom walked toward the front hall to see if the mailman had pushed any letters through the brass slot. I grinned at Gertie as we pulled our aprons off the hook. Wait till Mom saw! We both jumped as a scream came from the front of the house. Mom walked back to the kitchen fast.

"I don't have to ask whose idea that was," Mom said, looking at me. "Didn't I tell you not to touch those walls?"

"We didn't touch them, Mom, not with our fingers. We just decorated them with the crayons."

"Out! Out! I don't care if it is raining!"

We ran to get our coats. Mom pushed us onto the back porch and slammed the door behind us. Our list of weekly chores had just doubled.

A perfect house has so many rules: "Wipe your feet." "Stop that running!" "Don't touch the walls." "No yelling inside," as if the sound of our voices, like a wicked fairy godmother's spell, could undo Dad's promotion and plunk us back in our old house by the railroad tracks.

One summer morning we decided to see if Mom meant what she said about yelling. I filled a bucket with water, and Gertie got the soup ladle from the kitchen. We headed for the side porch, which, although attached to the house, was legally outdoors. We climbed onto the open railing between the pillars, counted to three, and began screaming our lungs out. No words, just screams that came from somewhere deep down inside. When we got thirsty, we ladled water from the bucket, took a swallow, and poured the rest over our faces. In between screaming jags, Gertie walked the railing like a tightrope acrobat, arms held out for balance, her red cowboy hat slung over her back.

Once, I turned to get a drink from the bucket and happened to glance into the porch window. Mom was standing behind the lace curtain. Uh-oh. But the corners of her mouth were turned up the tiniest bit, and her eyes looked past us to a place I couldn't see.

Gertie and I sat high on the rim of the abandoned quarry everyone called "the Ledge." The Ladies' Club was lunching at our house, and Mom had banished us until late afternoon. I used the wooden matches I'd taken from the kitchen drawer to light a fire—one of many we never told our parents about.

"When I grow up," Gertie said, "I'm going to have my own house and run all around in it and yell in it and never take a bath. When can I, Evie, when?"

I wasn't sure. Sometimes it was hard being the big sister. "You have to get married before you can have your own house," I said.

Gertie's face scrunched up with frustration.

"Come on," I said, jumping to my feet.

We ran around the top of the quarry, hopping from boulder to boulder, not being careful. Then we half-slid down the quarry's steep wall to visit our favorite cave—the one with the big red sign: "DO NOT ENTER." All the kids called the place "Hangman's Cave." Long ago an outlaw had hidden in the cave to escape from a posse. But the lawmen tracked him down, and a shooting match followed. When he ran out of bullets, the outlaw hanged himself.

The cool air inside the cave smelled of damp earth.

I patted the white leather belt of my Hopalong Cassidy double gun and holster set. If Gertie and I were out-laws, we would shoot our way out, not give up and hang ourselves just because the sheriff had us cornered.

One Saturday morning in August, there was an auction at old Mrs. Jensen's house on the corner. Mom had filled our house with antiques she'd bought for next to nothing at such auctions. She wanted to bid on the elm corner cupboard from Mrs. Jensen's dining room.

Gertie and I emptied our piggy banks. Total: fifty-three cents. We figured we could buy a lot for that, so we pulled our Red Flyer wagon behind us to Mrs. Jensen's house. The auctioneer was standing on a packing crate in the shade of the big oak tree. Furni-ture, card tables heaped with china and linens, and plain old junk crowded the yard from front to back. But there was only one thing Gertie and I wanted: a dreamy mountain of fat down pillows.

Mom was still behind the house looking at the furniture when the auctioneer asked, "Who'll start the bid for these pillows at fifty cents?"

Our whole stake! Up shot our arms.

"Fifty cents!" the auctioneer shouted, "Do I hear seventy-five?"

Gertie and I held our breath. If anyone else bid, we were finished.

"Fifty cents going once. . . . Going twice. . . . Sold!" called the auctioneer.

We couldn't believe our luck. Why hadn't anyone else bid on them? The grown-ups nudged each other and smiled as we paid our fifty cents and loaded the pillows into our wagon.

Gertie and I left the auction while Mom stayed to bid on the corner cupboard. When we got home we heaped the pillows on the living room rug and took turns throwing ourselves facedown into their softness. When we heard Mom open the back door, we ran to the kitchen and pulled her into the living room to see what we'd bought.

"Get those filthy things out of here!" she said. "What if there are lice in them?"

Gertie and I kind of shrunk up. We didn't look at each other as we carried the pillows down to the basement to await their trip to the dump.

That night when Mom gave us our bath, she scrubbed us harder than usual and soaped our hair twice. After we'd been put to bed, Gertie and I made a decision: We were going to run away from home.

The next morning, after a passing sprinkle of rain, there was a sign: A rainbow appeared in the sky south of town. We knew that if we followed it, we'd find the pot of gold and everything would be all right. We sneaked the pillows out of the basement and loaded them into the red wagon along with a paper bag full of cookies. We set out in the green morning air, heading toward one foot of the rainbow.

We walked for a long time—past white clapboard houses, their front porches curtained with roses; past side gardens of ripening tomatoes and onions; beyond the outskirts of town and along the cornfields on Holland Road—but we never seemed to get any closer to the rainbow. Thundery black clouds filled the sky. The rainbow disappeared, and fat raindrops mixed with hail pelted down. Gertie and I spotted an old maple tree in a field. We pulled the wagon as fast as we could under its shelter. I unloaded the pillows for us to sit on, but it was too late—they were wet, cold, and useless. Drenched and miserable, Gertie and I huddled under the tree.

After a while the rain stopped, but the rainbow never came back. Gertie pressed her lips together, determined not to be the first to cry, but her eyes brimmed with tears.

"Hey, Gertie, look!" I said, picking up some dirt and wiping it on my white blouse.

She stared at me in astonishment: Big Sister Defies Authority Again. After a moment, she smeared her own blouse, paused, and then threw a handful of dirt onto my shorts.

"Dirt fight!" I screamed.

We chased each other around and around the tree, laughing and shrieking, throwing dirt and weeds on each other. Then we flopped onto the wet ground and lay on our backs, breathing hard. The sun was just setting, and it was starting to get dark.

"I'm hungry," said Gertie.

We shared our last cookie. Our day of freedom had been sweet, even if we hadn't found the pot of gold. We stood for a silent moment looking down at our ruined pillows. Then we started back to town.

Gertie was so tired that I told her to get into the wagon and pulled her the rest of the way. She lay on her side dozing, with crumbs and dirt on her cheeks. When we got to the top of the Exchange Street hill, I woke her. Then I climbed into the wagon in front of her and steered us down the hill to our house, fast and dangerous, while Gertie held on to my waist from behind.

That gilded, perfect house on Exchange Street will always be a place of wonder and memory for me. But Gertie and I built another house for ourselves— as big as the whole town—filled with beauty, adventure, and the wildness of life. And in that house, we made our home.

—*Eve Powers*

# The Promise

The organist played a somber hymn as our procession filed into the small country church, following closely behind Carol's casket with the delicate rose etchings. The cold November wind whipped at our backs, making me shudder. My legs were numb, and the painful pinch of my new black pumps served as a reminder to place my feet carefully on the floor, slowing my pace. My arms draped around my children's shoulders, I steadied myself.

I kept my head high, eyes forward and focused on the altar in front, rather than on all the friends and relatives who watched as we passed. If I dared to look, I knew I'd find Carol's deadbeat ex-husband, sixteen-year-old Ashley's father.

Carol's nieces and nephews, a brother and sister-in-law, and her dad were there. All of them should have been stepping forward, taking control and offering comfort to Ashley. But they didn't. They were too wrapped up in their own lives. I didn't want to look at any of them. Not now. I only wanted to get through this day, if possible, without crying.

I took my place in the second row, behind Carol's family, with my children at my sides. The pew was hard and cold, like my pain. Muffled weeping filled the chilled air. The familiarity of the Catholic Mass was an odd comfort to me, even though I hadn't been to church since I was a girl. In a daze, I went along with the ritual. I stood when I was supposed to stand, sat when I was supposed to sit, all the while trying not to focus on Ashley's gut-wrenching sobs.

Carol and I had met as a result of our daughters' friendship. Our girls met when they were ten, at the horse stables where they took riding lessons. Soon, they were spending weekends together and calling each other daily to giggle about boys or clothes or whatever else young girls laugh about. Carol and I struck up our own friendship, and through our shared love of our daughters and horses, and then through sharing our deepest fears and secrets, hopes and dreams, we became like sisters. With our daughters, we were a fun foursome, spending most of our free time together—until Carol got sick.

Father Mulvaney, the priest conducting the Mass, said a lot of nice things about Carol during his homily. He spoke of Carol's love of life, her sense of right and wrong, and her untimely loss to cancer at the age of forty-five. I had met Father on several occasions over the past few weeks. He often came to Carol's bedside to counsel her on her journey ahead.

During his visits I would take a break, ducking outside for a cigarette or gathering the laundry and heading for the basement. I didn't want to participate in their visits, and I didn't listen in on their conversations. I knew Carol was mad at God. Frankly, so was I.

As the Mass neared the end, I remembered I had promised Carol I would sign the *Parish Book of Life* for her. The book was a remembrance of the parishioners whom the church had buried since its inception. I felt a wave of fear overtake me, knowing I would have to stand in front of all those people to fulfill my promise. My insides wrenched much like they had when, as a little girl, I was chosen to read my poem in front of the class. This time, though, the queasy feeling came not from the terror of being made fun of, but from something much more visceral . . . and powerful. And it was all I could do to hold myself together.

Too soon, Father Mulvaney made the announcement I had been dreading. Ashley's sobs grew louder. As I eased past my children and headed toward the priest, I didn't dare look back. A sense of panic set in, and I felt an urge to turn and bolt for the nearest exit. My heart was racing, pounding in my chest, heavy and labored with grief. I felt light-headed as I took the pen in my shaking right hand and searched for the heading in the book: November 11, 1999, the day my "sister" lost her battle with cancer.

The handwriting that followed was so scribbled I barely recognized it as my own. I placed the cap back on the pen and nodded to Father Mulvaney, gulping back my tears. At that moment I finally understood my panic. If I looked back at the faces of the other mourners, into their grief-stricken expressions, I would crumble.

I lowered my head, once again eyeing my painful new black pumps, and fumbled my way back to my place in the second row. When I returned to the cold, hard pew, I saw that while I'd been at the altar something wonderful had happened. Ashley had moved. She was seated next to my daughter. They were comforting each other. Ashley was becoming a part of us, just as her mother had requested.

Although the sight of them compounded my own grief and rattled my soul, I knew that falling apart was not an option for me. Not now. I had a job to do— one more promise to fulfill. It was time to give my "sister's" daughter a home and a family, picking up where Carol had left off. Ashley was coming to live with us, to be my daughter, to be my daughter's sister.

—Betsy O'Brien Harrison

# Tales of the Lawn Ranger

Before I knew it, I was a grown-up with a lawn of my own. My husband mowed it with his consumer-magazine-researched power mower. A sporty-looking thing: red and gray, reeking of gasoline and ear-blastingly loud. But efficient, of course. Very.

One day, in a yuppyish gardening catalog, I happened upon a person-powered push mower. My ears seemed to hum with the remembered long-ago gentle *whirring* of Dad's ancient push mower. In a flash I was a drowsy young girl, stretching and blinking awake to the sweet, green-scented promise of summer mornings. For a brief moment, I was sure that if I were to press my face to the window screen, as I did on those Saturday mornings of my childhood, I would see Dad following Rickety Green up and down the backyard as he shaved the lawn in methodical, overlapping stripes. It was irresistible, that memory, and soon a sleek reincarnation of Rickety Green squatted in our garage.

Each Saturday when my husband headed out to mow, I'd say, hopefully, "Are you going to use the new mower?"

Every Saturday he'd say, "I'm in a hurry today. Maybe next week."

It rained one weekend and the lawn couldn't be cut, and the next weekend we were out of town. One weekday morning, very early, I went out to look at the ankle-tickling tangle.

"Hmm," I said. Then a magnetic force yanked me toward the garage and the gleaming push mower.

It was a fight to the finish: teeth-gritted determination versus macraméd knots of vegetation. But in the end, I triumphed. I celebrated with a hot bath to soothe my shrieking muscles. That evening, as my husband admired my handiwork, I closed my fingers over my blistered palms and said, "Maybe I'll try it again next week."

The next time, mowing was easier. And I noticed things: new buds on the daylilies, the liquid warble of grosbeaks in the firs, a tree frog blinking at me from our cotoneaster. An orange and black butterfly drifted by. Wisps of cloud floated overhead. The scent of grass, my own personal aromatherapy, enveloped me. Shoving the mower, I felt an unaccustomed and joyful sensation of my own physical power.

I was hooked.

"You don't need to mow twice a week," my husband told me after I'd settled into a routine.

"Oh, yes," I said, discovering the truth as I spoke it. "Yes, I do."

My sister, who lives too far away (I only hope she says the same about me), and I got together. We were catching up, talking about what we'd been doing for fun.

"I mow the lawn." I felt foolish saying it.

My sister's eyebrows disappeared into her hairline. She blinked her incredible hazel eyes at me and opened and closed her mouth a couple of times.

"Uh," I said. "With a push mower like Dad had once—remember?"

She nodded vigorously and in a kind of dazzled wonder said, "I do, too. With a push mower."

Then she told me a story. It seems a coworker of her husband's came into work one morning laughing and shaking his head. He said to Mike, "Come take a little ride. I'm gonna show you something you won't believe."

To my brother-in-law's amazement, he was driven straight to his own neighborhood and slowly past his own yard, where my sister was shaving their acre of lawn in careful whirring strips.

"Can you beat that?" the coworker said. "I didn't even know they still made those things. Who on

Earth do you think she is? Does she have a clue this is the twentieth century?"

All my sister's husband could say was, "Uh, well, actually . . ."

In the midst of our laughter, I almost asked her if mowing had become for her, like it was for me, a kind of meditation. If, while she watches the grass change from shag to velvet, she also watches memories and daydreams play in the theater of her mind. If ideas and plans and possibilities swirl by her, some worth catching. If she finds herself, as she shoves the mower up and down, also pushing backward and forward into her own yesterdays and tomorrows.

I almost asked her, but I didn't. Because somehow, in that unspoken way of sisters, I didn't need to.

—*Terry Miller Shannon*

This story was published as "A Time Machine That Also Cuts Grass" in the *Christian Science Monitor*, October 23, 1997.

# Not Only My Sister

"Wake up and play with me," I whined, shaking my sister.

She kept lying there in her twin-sized bed, snoring softly. So I pinched her, just a little.

"Ouch," she jumped. "Why did you do that?"

"Because I need you to wake up and draw rainbows with me," I said matter-of-factly.

"I'm too sleepy right now," she said and went back to sleep.

I stomped away and flopped onto my own bed, pouting and plotting. I'd teach her.

Jessica and I did everything together—wherever I went, she was right behind me; whenever I did six-year-old, big-girl things, she tried her five-year-old best to do the same. Even though I was only ten months older, she listened to me and let me boss her around. She often told me I was the smartest sister in the whole wide world, stretching her arms out on both sides to demonstrate just how big the world is.

I sat on my bed, my feet dangling over the side, grumbling to myself. This was so unfair. Mama told me she was having me a little sister so I could have someone to play with. But my sleepy-headed sister was no fun at all.

I decided that when she woke up, I would draw by myself and I wouldn't be her sister anymore. I sat at the Little Princess desk we shared and pulled out my construction paper, a pencil, and crayons and began to draw my rainbows.

I sighed in exasperation. This was getting boring quickly. Without Jessica, I had no one to draw me a nice big sun to go with my rainbow. Frustrated, I tossed the crayons onto the floor and tore the construction paper in half. I bit the eraser off the pencil, spit it into my hand, and looked at it slyly. Smiling to myself, I crept over to my sister's bed and slipped the tiny eraser into her ear, pushing it in deeply with my pinky finger. That would show her.

When Jessica woke up later that day, we played together and I forgot all about the tiny eraser nub I'd shoved into her ear.

Days later we were in our room playing Barbies when our mother called out, "Tamekia! Jessica! Dinner is ready."

I jumped to my feet, ready to go, but Jessica just sat

there and continued to play as if she hadn't heard a thing. I nudged her. She looked up, and I grabbed her hand and led her to the kitchen table. Over dinner Mom talked to us and asked about our school day. I eagerly told her about how my teacher, Ms. Sampson, had praised my reading and given me a gold star.

"What about you, Jessica?" Mom asked.

I glanced over at my sister, watching as she continued to shovel rice into her mouth, as if not a word had been spoken.

"Jessica," my mother called, her voice rising slightly. Jessica looked up, her almond-shaped eyes widening. "Didn't you hear me talking to you?" my mother asked, her voice gentle and calm.

"No, ma'am," my little sister said.

"Mama, she did that earlier, too," I stated in my Ms. Know-It-All voice. "When you called us for dinner, she just sat there like she didn't even hear you. I had to make her get up."

Mom started to do something she called "testing Jessica's hearing." She went into different rooms and called out or made noise and asked me if Jessica reacted. It became quite clear that Jessica was having problems with her hearing. Later that night I lay awake in my bed, wondering what the doctor would tell us and what was wrong with my little sister.

"Hop on up here, Jessica," Dr. Wells said in a jolly voice, reminding me of Santa.

"What seems to be the problem, Ms. Jones?"

"Well, it seems as though Jessica is having prob-lems hearing. She doesn't respond unless we speak very loudly."

"Well, let's see what we have here," Dr. Wells mumbled to Jessica, walking over to her with a silver thing. He put it in Jessica's ear, pressed a button, and gazed in intently.

Alarmed, I shouted, "What are you doing to my sister?"

Chuckling to himself, the doctor said, "I'm not hurting her. I'm checking to see whether there is something lodged in your sister's ear."

"Oh, okay. Go ahead."

After looking for a few more moments, he said, "I think I see the problem."

He reached over and picked up a small silver thing that looked like long scissors with a clamp at the end. As he slowly put it into Jessica's ear, I winced.

"Here we go," he said, and pulled out a small pink nub in the clamp of the silver thing.

My eyes got big as saucers as I realized that the reason my little sister hadn't been able to hear was because she had an eraser in her ear—an eraser I'd put there.

"Did you put this in your ear, Jessica?" Dr. Wells asked in his doctor's voice.

"No, sir," she mumbled, her lower lip trembling.

I looked down sheepishly, knowing she was about to cry, knowing it was my fault.

Dr. Wells stepped over to me and lifted up my chin. "Did you put this eraser in your sister's ear?"

"Yes," my voice cracked, tears streaming down my puffed-up cheeks.

Jessica's eyes narrowed as she looked at me, hurt and anger flashing in them.

"Why would you do that, Tamekia?" the doctor inquired.

Sniffling, I rambled, "Because when mommy got pregnant I thought I was going to have a sister to play with and we'd do everything together. It's always supposed to be Tamekia and Jessica, right?" Not waiting for a reply, I rushed on in my high-pitched voice. "But it's not like that. Jessica doesn't want to play with me anymore. She's mean to me. She isn't my sister anymore."

"But I am your sister. I'll always be your sister," Jessica said.

She scooted and wiggled, trying to get off the doctor's table without falling. Dr. Wells scooped her up and planted her on the floor. She walked over and hugged me and said, "Not only are you my sister, you are my best friend."

And that's what we've been ever since.

—Tamekia Reece

# Home Away from Home

Life for me was great. I had two indulgent older brothers and an adoring sister, Elma, who was the eldest. I lived in the country in an old farmhouse in Scotland, and the fields and lanes were my playing grounds. One sunny summer day when I was ten, I skipped my way home and found my uncle standing in our doorway and my aunt crying in his arms.

The older of my two brothers, John, walked toward me, and I knew from his manner that something horrendous had happened. Tears streaked his face and his voice cracked as he told me, "Oh, Julia, Mum's had a terrible accident. She's fallen, and . . . and she landed very badly."

Frowning, I asked, "Is she going to the hospital?"

My aunt put her arms around me and said gently, "Julia, sweetheart, you have to be brave. Mummy's gone to be with God."

I knew what that meant: My mum had died. I was devastated and couldn't believe such an awful thing could happen to us. Didn't we pray at every meal and bedtime? Didn't we read the Bible and do our best to live by the Gospel? Didn't we go to church every Sunday?

When the tears finally subsided, I looked at my brothers and asked, "What will happen to us?"

For now we were orphans. Dad had died when I was five. Our older sister, Elma, lived all the way across the ocean in America, and my brothers were still in high school. To my surprise, Elma arrived home from the States that very afternoon.

She sat me on her knee and said, "Julia, I want you to come home to Galena with me."

"Are we all coming to live with you?" I asked.

She bit her lip and said, "No, Bill and I can't look after you all. John is going to university and will live with some friends. Aunt and Uncle will look after Stephen."

I was so upset at the thought of being separated from my brothers that I suppose I was quite difficult. But Elma had endless patience with me, and my brothers told me it was a great thing and reassured me they would come visit me in Iowa.

I don't remember much of the flight, other than crying and feeling sleepy. I remember awakening in Galena, and thinking it looked nothing like Chicago or

New York, which was all I knew of America, from television programs and movies. Though I liked those films, I didn't much fancy living in a big city, having lived in the Scottish countryside. So, when Elma showed me around Galena and I saw how quaint it was, with the river and ducks and Grant Park, and the lovely old shops and surrounding countryside, I felt somewhat relieved.

We lived a little way out of town on the route to Dubuque. Bill grew corn rather than potatoes, but the fields and trees and rolling hills looked almost like home. I started thinking that maybe I could live happily there after all.

Of course, I faced many changes and challenges in my new life: the way I spoke and looked, new friends, different lessons at school. Elma helped me tremendously. She took time off work to spend time with me, introducing me to kids my age, picking me up from school until I felt confident enough to take the school bus, teaching me about American kids and customs. Her two children were very young, but they had obviously been coached to make me welcome, and I grew to love them quickly.

Elma also comforted me through my lonely nights, when I cried for my mum and my brothers. As soon as she and Bill could afford it, they paid for Stephen to come over to visit.

As I grew into my teens, I shared all my secrets

with Elma, telling her sisterly things I probably would never have told Mum—like about boys I fancied. She made my whole life easier.

When I was twenty-two, I met Chris and fell head over heels in love. We married two years later. Bill gave me away, and Elma was my matron of honor. Not long after our honeymoon, Chris and I moved to Chicago, and Elma came to help shop for things for our apartment. Within the year, to our delight, we were expecting our first child, and when little Caroline was born, Elma was there to help me through that, too. One day during her visit, over glasses of iced tea while Caroline napped, I told Elma how much I loved her and how grateful I was for all she'd done for me since I'd arrived as a woeful ten-year-old.

"You have been both sister and mother to me."

"Julia . . . ," she began, then bit her lip. "Julia . . . that is what I am—your mother and your sister."

"I know," I said, smiling. "You're a wonderful sister, and you've been just like a mother to me."

"No, Julia. What I'm trying to say is, I *am* your mother. I'm your birth mother."

I stared in disbelief as Elma explained how she'd given birth to me when she was only sixteen. The father had run off as soon as he'd learned she was pregnant. Our mum offered to raise me as her own child, and Elma had agreed, believing it was best for me. Then, when she was nineteen, Elma had met Bill and gone to live in America.

"You were just three then, and though I loved you and knew I'd miss you terribly, I felt that you were Mum's baby, not mine," she explained. "After I had my other two children, I thought about you even more, wondered what you were like, what made you laugh and cry.

"When Mum died," she continued, "I couldn't wait to bring you home with us, to give you all the love and care I hadn't been able to the first ten years of your life. So many times, I wanted to tell you, but I didn't have the courage, for fear of hurting or losing you."

Still reeling, I could only hug her and weep. We both cried. Finally, I found the words I wanted and needed to say.

"You've never hurt me, and you will never lose me, Elma. You have shown me only love, and your love has always been a soothing balm for the hurts in my life," I said gently. "Thank you, Sister, for caring for me like a mother. Thank you, Mom, for sharing everything with me like a sister."

—*Joyce Stark, as told by Julia Crawford*

# Psychic Sisters' Hotline

"Who else could buy you underwear?" my sister, Margery, asked, handing me a Lands' End three-pack of high-cut cotton briefs in white and baby blue. "But as well as Lands' End fits"—her voice ran up the scale, then paused for effect as she whipped out a pair of black cotton, five percent spandex undies from a plastic bag—"these Balis fit even better."

Of course, she was right. My sister and I have the same shape, smaller versions of our mother's hourglass figure. Okay, hour and a half.

Because Margery loves to shop, she's my scout. Years ago, when we were both in New York visiting Mom, Margery called from Syms, where she was rummaging the racks of that discount mecca the size of two football fields.

"Get in the car and drive here immediately," she commanded. "They have pants that fit us. Norton

McNaughton, small waist, big hips. I take a twelve; you'll take a ten."

A few weeks later, when she was back home in Wisconsin and I was home in California, she alerted me by cell: "I'm at the Lands' End outlet. They have cotton twill capris on sale, thirty-five percent off. Do you want me to get you a pair in midnight blue? They're irregular. I'll have to try on twenty pairs, but I'm willing to do it. Mom is ecstatic. She just found a windbreaker, price slashed to $16.99, then discounted another forty percent."

My sister and I are like twins separated at birth. Six years and 2,000 miles apart, we have a spooky psychic connection, most evident in matters of retail. Make that wholesale.

The first documented event was about twenty-five years ago, when my sister showed up in California with the same weird collapsible hairbrush that I had just purchased on impulse on my way back from Tahoe one hot summer night. The next time I visited her in Milwaukee, I couldn't wait to recommend my new SAS sandals. I knew she would thank me forever for saving her aching tootsies. When she picked me up at the airport, she was wearing the very same sandals.

We buy the same brand of Zen green tea and the same bras, sliders for furniture, and cup holders for cars—sometimes on the same day, without prior knowledge of the other's latest find.

On one of our sprees in Milwaukee's Marshalls, after separately filling our carts, she called over the dressing booth's plywood partition, "Laur, you should try this on. It might look good on you."

I replied, "And this might be good on you."

Unlatching the locks on our flimsy booth doors, we stepped into the neon fluorescent corridor and saw our mirror image. We were both trying on the same cinnamon silk shift.

When we're together we burst into the same song, at the same moment, on the same note. We convulse with laughter at the same sound or sight— a primordial laughter that bubbles from a place so deep, it's an instinctive physical response, barely filtering through our brains.

Recently, as we took our balcony seats for a concert version of *The Flying Dutchman*, she whispered, "They should have told us the light bar would obstruct our view."

"It doesn't matter," I whispered back. "The acoustics are good."

When the tenor took his place, an enormous black rectangular box hanging over the stage blocked his face like a censor's black bar hiding porno body parts. We cracked up in decorous Davies Hall, each clapping a hand over our mouth, fluttering the other, limp-wristed and hysterical, in an effort to stifle our giggles.

We share memories that trigger exactly the same mental picture or reaction. How Daddy's green bathing suit, made of a nylon so indestructible he wore it for thirty years, ballooned like pontoons around his hips when he waded into the pool. Mom leading us like ducklings across Delancey Street, loaded down with bags of skirts, blouses, shoes, and underwear on our annual shopping pilgrimage to the Lower East Side. Our brother, Danny, banging out chords on the piano in our Long Island childhood living room, writhing in his James Brown imitation, while my sister and I sang backup: Danny and the Deutschettes.

She was my worshipful baby sister, my roommate from the time she was three and I was nine, until I left for college. When she was in elementary school, she would try on my persona for size, slinging my purse over her shoulder, carrying my schoolbooks up the stairs to our room. At night after lights-out, I entertained her with stories or shadow puppet shows on the wall behind our twin beds, where the light from the school across the street cast our puppet stage. We laughed and talked until Dad yelled down the hall, "You girls better get to sleep in there!" We never turned in without our "kiss, hug, and secret" ritual—the secret a whispered "I love you" when we had nothing juicier to share.

This sister thing goes deeper than secrets and laughter, deeper than shared history and gene pool.

Although she's the younger, apparently we got switched in our cradles, because when we grew up, she became "the boss."

On her last visit to San Francisco, for a conference, she came without her husband and son. A sister week. Within minutes of arriving she was on a ladder in my study changing the smoke alarm battery, replacing the defective garden hose, shopping for cushions for my patio furniture, introducing me to the miracle of Febreze to kill the smell in the suitcase stored in my garage, editing my latest magazine queries and essays, and issuing directives.

"Send the queries to *Oprah*, the essay to *Vanity Fair*. If you offered me a million dollars, I couldn't write this," she praised me. She offers me her energy, her advice, her care.

"Neither of us lives near family," she said. "It's not right. You should sell your house and move to Milwaukee."

"There's this thing that happens in Milwaukee," I said. "I think you call it winter. Personally, I like a four-degree temperature range, between sixty-eight and seventy-two, perfect for a hothouse flower like me."

"You could sell your house for a bundle and buy one in Wisconsin for much less. You wouldn't have to work." She was pulling out the stops.

"You could come to Eli's games and school plays." She played her ace, knowing I adore her son, now ten years old. "And you could pick him up after school and chauffeur him around." The double edge of living nearby.

I had flown to Milwaukee every month or two during Eli's first two years to bond and experience the joy of this gifted, old-soul child.

"I had him for both of us," she'd told me.

To him, she had said, "I'm Mommy Number One; she's Mommy Number Two."

From his infancy, Eli noticed the "sister stereo effect." Seated in his blue high chair at the kitchen table, listening to us sing "La Bamba," our voices the same timbre and intonation, his tiny head swiveled from her to me and back. His full lips pursed, he stared at me with gray-green saucer eyes with a look I like to remember as the perfect blend of love and awe.

How could I not live near that?

Periodically, I weigh the options. Mill Valley . . . Milwaukee. Hiking along a stream in the redwood grove behind my home . . . trudging on a treadmill, slip-sliding on an icy sidewalk trying to get to my car.

Mill Valley . . . Milwaukee. My attachments here . . . my sister there.

I love the Mill Valley home I designed and built on a hill overlooking San Francisco Bay. How do I balance my friendships, knit and purled over thirty years of living here, against my love for Margery—my confidante, style consultant, story editor, shopping guru, travel companion, diet partner, joke feeder, best friend, and mother of the child I never had?

Maybe some day my sister and I will have adjoining rooms in the nursing home. For now, we'll make do with calls, visits, and our psychic sisters' hotline, sharing deep laughter and underwear tips.

—*Laura Deutsch*

# The Magical Bond of Alexabeth

My husband knew before I did that I was pregnant. He walked out of the bathroom cradling the plastic square in the palm of his hand, his eyes shell-shocked but his face glowing. I was sitting on the couch, pretending to read a magazine, when he walked into the living room.

"It's got a pink cross on it," he said, holding it up for me to see.

I knew one line meant negative and two meant positive. A cross was two lines. We were going to have a baby!

The excitement of that moment held until six months later, when Tim and I went to the clinic for an ultrasound. I followed the instructions and drank four glasses of water and then struggled to lie flat on the cold hard table, my bladder feeling as if it might burst. The weight of the technician's arm, which he carelessly rested on my mountain of a tummy, was almost more than I could bear. *A-B-C, 1-2-3. A-B-C, 1-2-3*, I repeated silently, staring straight up at the ceiling, trying to distract myself from thinking about my bladder.

Finally, the technician said casually, "Well, I see why you're so big: You've got two babies in there."

Without thinking, I reached over and grabbed the technician by his starched white collar and pulled him toward me so fast he didn't have time to wipe the smirk off his face before it was inches from mine. With narrowed eyes and clenched teeth, I spat out, "That's not funny, mister. Don't you ever joke with a pregnant woman."

"I'm not joking. You're having twins," he said, as calmly as if he had just told me I was having spaghetti for dinner.

My panic subsided slightly when I looked over at Tim. He is British and usually quite reserved, but upon hearing the news, he balled his hand into a fist and pumped it against his knee, hissing, "*Yes!*"

Without much discussion, we decided to find out the babies' genders. The technician told us in the same spaghetti-dinner tone that one was positively a girl, the other was maybe a girl, but he couldn't be sure. While my mind spun with visions of two car seats, two cribs, and two highchairs, I heard my husband murmur, "Two college educations, two weddings."

The babies were due in three months, but we were told to expect them at least a month early. That left only two months to prepare for two babies instead of one. I devoured every book I could on twin births and contacted the local Mothers of Multiples club. My husband walked around telling everyone he was "Super Sperm."

As my stomach quickly grew beyond the cute basketball shape, the equipment and baby clothes in our third-floor apartment grew by the same leaps and bounds. Upon hearing our news, friends and family showered us with gifts of matching outfits, from newborn to preteen size. Our small apartment was loaded with baby gear, and we felt ready—except for the names.

When we'd thought we were having one baby, choosing a name had been part of our evening entertainment. Romantic and dreamy sometimes, it was a democratic process always. We'd each write down our favorite names and compare them; if we both liked a name, it was upgraded to finalist status. Then we'd cross-examine every finalist name, digging deep to root out any that reminded us of ex-girlfriends and ex-boyfriends. After weeks of playing this game, we agreed on Elizabeth for a girl and Alexander for a boy. We began calling the baby inside my tummy "Alexabeth."

But after the ultrasound, we were thrown back into the baby-naming routine. We needed another girl's name. We dug out the lists and started again, but this time we didn't have the luxury of time to ponder their meanings. We took a shortcut and decided the name Alexander would be changed to Alexandra for a girl. This fit nicely, because we'd chosen the name Elizabeth for Queen Elizabeth, and though I'd lived in London for only a year and had never seen the queen in person, I'd had the pleasure of meeting a princess named Alexandra.

I received loads of advice from books and friends on how to have a good hospital experience when giving birth. Some of it I discarded summarily, but one suggestion I was determined to carry out was to keep my babies with me and out of the nursery as much as possible. I wanted to bond with them from the minute they were born. My wishes were granted, and the two bassinets were in my room, side by side, as often as allowed. For most of our hospital stay the girls were snuggled in their bassinets, wrapped tightly in soft blankets, wearing tiny white knit caps with pink bows.

On the day we were to leave the hospital, we dressed the girls in white sleepers with yellow ducks. It was an emotional time, knowing we were leaving the safety net of the nursing staff and venturing out on our own as new parents. I had dreamed of this idyllic moment, but the girls did not like being put into clothing. They fussed and cried. Tim held one and I held the other. Then we'd switch. We walked, rocked, and bounced. But nothing we did soothed them. They just cried that brittle newborn cry and clumsily waved their arms around.

"Lin, what should we do?" Tim asked.

"I don't know. I really don't know," I said.

As if giving up, we both laid the girls down on the bed. Suddenly, their arms stopped waving. Their bodies stopped wiggling. Their cries stopped. We stared at them in amazement, as they grew completely still and silent. Then, with the slightest movement, Elizabeth moved her head over to Alexandra at the same time Alexandra moved her head closer to Elizabeth. Elizabeth opened her eyes and stared at her sister's face. Alexandra kept her eyes closed, but snuggled closer to her sister and a peaceful look came over her face.

I stood there feeling like an outsider. The comfort my husband and I had been unable to give them, they'd found in each other. The moment we laid them side by side on the bed, they immediately felt each other's presence. As I watched their bodies relax, I realized that the bond they shared as sisters was stronger than anything I had ever witnessed or experienced. A chill shot through me, and I shivered.

Elizabeth and Alexandra had been together in my womb from the beginning. Only after they were born were they separated by blankets and bassinets, unable to feel and hear each other. My heart ached at how scared and lonely those first days apart must have been for them, perhaps wondering where the other had gone.

When I think back to that day, when our daughters first showed me the bond they share, I smile, but I don't remind them of it. Right now, they are busy growing up as sisters—competing for parental attention, fighting over the remote, wondering who ate all the Golden Grahams, and complaining that life isn't fair. But when I see them pass to each other on the soccer field or take turns singing the Sandy part in "Summer Nights," or when tears well up in one's eyes when the other is sad or she writes a sappy letter to the one who's away at camp, my mind goes back to that day. The day my "Alexabeth" became Alexandra and Elizabeth and my newborn daughters unknowingly taught me that a sister's love starts in the womb.

—*Linda Today Robinson*

# Throwing My First Homer

There I stood on the dusty field. Wearing my sisters' hand-me-down jeans with the hole where the pocket used to be and my brother's dyed yellow T-shirt. Standing in the schoolyard with the rest of the kids, waiting to be picked. Eager for my last chance before summer vacation to show the world what I was made of.

Danny Homer was one of the captains, and I knew he wouldn't pick me. He still hadn't forgiven me for attempting to bribe him into an early marriage in front of the whole fourth-grade class. My sister Jeanette was in charge of the other team, and I figured family honor must count for something. Still, I detected an evil gleam in her eye as she surveyed the runny-nosed and scraped-kneed offerings on the playground, big and small, hopefuls like me.

My sister was in grade seven, the head honcho,

the big cheese, the position we all aspired to. But soon she would have to endure the torturous bus trip to the junior high in the big town of Kindersley, with the farting boys and the miles and miles of dusty road separating her from the safety of our family farm. Danny would be there, making her life hell, rubbing it in that he was always a mark above her in sports and how she'd blown her chance for the all-stars last summer. Soon, she would be at the bottom of the heap. I snickered. Then I gulped. Had I talked about it?

I did sort of recall saying something like, "You think you're so big and important, you just wait and see!" And so what if I did coerce my older sisters into relating their horror stories of eighth grade. I might even have made up a few stories myself, borrowed from friends whose older siblings had walked the halls with "Kick me" signs on their backs. She couldn't still be mad about that, could she?

It is never easy being the last one picked. It was bad enough to be the last one in our family, the youngest of five that stretched from my eldest sister, Cathy, down past Pat, past Jeanette—who now held my future ball career in her hands—to my next in line, my one and only brother, Ken, whose sole purpose in life was to torment me daily.

Jeanette eyed me over and smiled, then pointed. I leapt up, and then realized she was pointing behind me. Only a few of us remained on the field—the unchosen. Now I knew how the rookies felt at draft pick. I sighed. I smiled. I promised God things I could never deliver even if I wanted to and some I certainly didn't want to.

Danny picked next: the kid with the Coke-bottle glasses. Then Jeanette went, passing over cross-eyed Clarence and me for the Portuguese kid who didn't speak English. I was doomed. I was going to be last, again.

Then, a miracle happened. One of the boys whispered in Danny's ear, and low and behold, he picked me! I wasn't the last one left on the field, after all. I was going to play. Strut my stuff. Show that mean, stuck-up, so-and-so sister of mine a thing or two. She would rue the day she didn't pick me.

My sister was pitching the first round. This was not good. My sister had a hardball that shook the paint off the sides of houses when it whipped by. Many a bruise on our legs and chest were grim reminders of when Jeanette threw too close to the mound. In the aggressive "call ya yeller chicken" world of prairie baseball, no one would think twice if you declined to bat first against Hardball Netty Marples.

It was decided that, because I was a relative and blood was thicker than water, I should go first. I guessed Danny figured Jeanette would never seriously hurt one of her own. The broken arm my brother had gotten last year on this very field must

Jeanette just looked straight ahead. Then she smiled smugly. Uh-oh, I was going to get it now.

"Yep, no one can toss a bat like my sister," she said. "Man, you shoulda seen the look on Loud Mouth Danny's face when that bat came at him. It was awesome! He'll probably be in the hospital a whole week. That'll keep him out of the playoffs at school.

"That was awesome," she repeated. Then she slugged me in the arm for old times' sake.

After dishes, Jeanette took me out in the backyard to teach me how to throw hardballs. I broke two windows that summer and had the time of my life. Danny never picked me again, for baseball or matrimony, and he kept out of the way whenever Nancy Wild Swing Marples was up to bat.

*—Nancy Bennett*

# A Poet Lives Here

Barring the first fourteen months of my life before her birth, she has always been my best friend, my confidante, an extension of myself. So I thought I knew my sister better than anyone else in the world. That is, until the evening of her fortieth birthday.

Traditionally, my sister and I treat each other to a sisters-only birthday dinner on our special day. On the eve of her big four-oh, we shared pasta, salad, and a glass of wine at our favorite Italian restaurant. Afterward, while driving her home, she nonchalantly pointed out a gabled stone cottage.

"That has always been my favorite house," she said. "Wouldn't it be heaven to actually live in such a place?"

Then she sighed. "And that beautiful basket of white and yellow flowers hanging on the door. Have you ever seen anything so enchanting?"

Her gushing over the house made me nearly miss the next turn. Not that the house wasn't lovely; I just never would have expected my sister to appreciate it. And I wondered, do I know her at all? Oblivious to my shock, she slid back into her normal chatter about her three kids, her crazy dog, and her husband's accounting practice as if she hadn't just said the most uncharacteristic thing I'd ever heard her say.

As I maneuvered the car into her asphalt driveway, the dog was digging in the lawn, my nephew was bouncing a basketball, my nieces were sitting on the curb, and every light in the house seemed to be burning. Her sports utility vehicle was safely encased in the garage. Life in suburbia. After a quick hug of thanks, she jumped out of my car and was swallowed up by the domestic chaos that seemed to define her life for the past seventeen years.

On my way home, I backtracked to the quiet street where the stone cottage seemed almost nestled into the landscape. Tranquil, so unlike my sister's home. The cobbled driveway curved and flared. A sundial surrounded by beautiful shrubbery was tucked into a corner of the property, where a scalloped birdbath offered refreshment for a pair of cardinals. Six graceful gables provided a charming silhouette against the evening sky, and the lovely flowers that seemed to dance in the basket hanging on the front door provided the finishing touch.

Looking closer, I discovered the basket contained at least a dozen silk daffodils, and I imagined their yellow and white petals bending as the door swung open, as if bowing in welcome to visitors. The cottage did seem enchanted, and suddenly I felt ashamed of myself. Why wouldn't my sister crave such a peaceful setting? Why had I assumed that her standard four-bedroom Colonial, three rambunctious kids, and an erratic dog were her entire perception of the American dream?

Oh, don't misunderstand me. She'd never forfeit the life she has chosen; she loves her children, her husband, her home, even that crazy dog. What distressed me was that I wasn't more in sync with her yearnings, her dreams. I remembered that as a teen she shunned the typical young adult novels and romances, preferring to spend her time reading poetry and clipping quotations. I thought she might someday write her own volume of reflections. Now, I wondered, where was that creative, artistic young woman? Did she get lost somewhere between motherhood and her fortieth birthday?

The following day I stopped at a local florist. I selected a delicate basket and a full bouquet of silk daffodils, white and yellow.

"I'd like you to fill this basket with these flowers. They need to be arranged as artistically as possible. They're for someone very special."

The florist smiled. "This daffodil is called *Narcissus poeticus*. It has been revered by writers and poets throughout the ages."

"Actually," I said, "the person they're for used to dabble in poetry, although she has yet to complete a single poem. I guess life sometimes gets in the way."

"Ah! Then these are perfect," he said, placing the finished basket in my hands. "*Poeticus* is the last flower in the *Narcissus* family to bloom. Unlike the other hardy daffodils that take on the winds of March, this one waits for calm weather and rarely blooms until April, sometimes even May. But when it does bloom, it is magnificent."

Suddenly, I understood. Like *Narcissus poeticus*, my sister had bided her time, gathering her resources and nurturing her creativity. As I carefully placed the basket in the trunk of my car, I couldn't help smiling. Somehow, I knew it was her time to bloom.

—*Barbara Davey*

# Little Black Cat

They live in nursing homes on opposite sides of the country. They used to write to each other, but now neither can remember if the other is still living or whether they are young or old. They live mostly in a time gone by, when they were young and happy.

Irene, the older sister, is nearing ninety. When she was a young widow, she drove her nine-year-old daughter to Northern California to make a new life. The trip took four days. Now, she can no longer live alone. She has fallen and broken bones and is often confused. The last time I saw her, she held a pile of unopened birthday cards on her lap, fingering the envelopes she had received a week earlier. She had forgotten her own birthday.

Lucille, the younger one, is my mother. She has lived all her life in the mill town where they were born. She worked hard in factories, weaving carpets, sewing uniforms, or stitching basketballs. In those years her hands were rough and red. Now they are soft as she fingers the edges of her blanket. I wheel her chair to the sunroom on the fourth floor. She is examining the blanket's stitching, looking for mistakes, as though she were back at work. I tell her I have seen Irene, and she smiles. I know what's coming, and I sit back and listen as she tells the story.

In the 1920s, they were little girls, the daughters of parents who had left Poland at the dawn of the twentieth century to come to America. Grandma and Grandpa Smitka made their way by train from Ellis Island to a crowded factory town on the Mohawk River in northern New York State. Their first child, a daughter born when Grandma was only a girl herself at seventeen, died in infancy from influenza. Irene was born a few years later, in 1911, and Lucille came along three years after that. Four more children quickly followed, and though all were well loved, their parents' time was hard to come by. Grandpa worked in a broom factory and later a butcher shop. There was no automatic washing machine or dishwasher, no self-cleaning oven or even hot running water. Grandma had her hands full, and Irene and Lucille often took care of the little ones. Irene, the oldest and, according to Lucille, the bossiest, held authority over the other children, but most of the chores fell to Lucille.

When Irene was a toddler, a bout with polio left her "crippled." She limped in her heavy brown shoes, and she often fell when she tried to run. So her second-in-line sister, Lucille, was the one who wheeled the babies in their carriage, fed them, and washed their little dresses. She was the one Grandma sent to the store for a last-minute loaf of bread or a bottle of milk. Sometimes, in that busy household, Irene felt she was in the way, with nothing to contribute. Since she was excused from most of the work, she had lots of time to read and study, and so she became "the clever one" in the family. On the day of Mom's never-forgotten story, Irene performed a bit of the magic that only big sisters can.

Lucille was at the kitchen table working on a school project, a pen-and-ink drawing. Her dark brown eyes concentrated on the precious sheet of white paper. There was only one piece and no extra for mistakes. She worked for hours, creating a scene of the creek where all the children played. Just as she was finishing, a drop of ink fell from her pen and landed at the bottom of her drawing.

Heartbroken, Lucille began to cry so loudly she alarmed her big sister, who was reading in the next room. Irene couldn't run like the others, but she could get around fast enough when she wanted to. Her heavy leg thumped on the wooden floor as she hurried to the kitchen table.

"Luca, what's the matter?" she asked, using her pet name for her sister.

Lucille wiped her wet face with her sleeve. She sniffed and moved away from the table, so that Irene could see what had happened.

"Give me the pen," was all Irene said.

Irene's dark brown curls fell over her face as she bent over the drawing. Holding her locks back with one hand, with her other she carefully dipped the pen into the blob of ink. Using the sharp point, Irene slowly pulled out a pair of tiny feet, then a head with two pointy ears, and finally, as Lucille watched spellbound, a long and curving tail. Irene had transformed the ugly ink spot into a perky black cat!

More than seventy years have come and gone, but Lucille, my mother, still remembers. Mom doesn't stay long in the present anymore, and she may not recall your name. But ask her about Irene and her eyes sparkle.

"It was like magic," she says, her eyes shining as she tells the tale.

Then she smiles to herself with the smile of the girl she was, warmed by the memory of a sister's love and the magic that turned tears into laughter.

—*Linda C. Wisniewski*

This story was published in *Mocha Memoirs*, Volume 5, Issue 8.

# Breathe

"Amy." The whisper came out of the dark, the tone beseeching. "Amy, are you awake? Can I come sleep with you?"

"Yeah, come on."

I slid over to the cold spot on the sheets, and my sister slipped into the warm hollow I had vacated. She sighed, I don't know whether from satisfaction in getting the warm spot or with relief from escaping whatever terror had driven her from her bed to mine.

She is a year older than me, almost exactly. If we had both been born on our due dates, we would have been birthday twins. As it was, people often thought we were twins, which always made me laugh. I've always thought of us as photo negatives of each other: She's dark; I'm light. She's tall; I'm short. She's artistic; I'm logical.

I looked over at her familiar presence, her pink

sponge-rollered head, covered by a granny cap, resting on my pillow. I never understood her fear. Sometimes, it was the fear of dying.

What made her think about these things? We were eleven and twelve years old. I thought we were immortal. I believed that the simple act of reaching up from my trundle bed and holding her hand could conquer all the terrors of the night. She, however, saw things I never saw. Even my most vivid imaginings could not compare to the images that manifested themselves to Beth. She did not have nightmares; she had hallucinations. My night world was far more pedestrian, and the solace I could offer my sister was to share my bed and talk about a death I did not believe would come for decades. It was easy enough for me to convince her that, as long as we were breathing in the morning, it was safe to get up and start our day. Day by day, just get up and breathe.

Beth married young. Her first son, Nick, was born when she was eighteen. By the time she was twenty-five, she had two more sons, Alex and Noah.

One morning shortly after Noah's birth, I was startled by my ringing phone. It was 5:45 A.M. Though I was awake, the sound frightened me and filled me with dread. My heart made a free fall into the pit of my stomach and lay there like a lead weight. My mother's voice over the telephone line sounded thin, frightened.

"Amy, something terrible has happened—" her voice choked off, more like a gag than a sob. "I can't say it."

"Mom, who? What?" I have a large family and the thought of anything happening to any of them terrified me, but I had to know.

"I can't say the words—" her voiced trailed off.

"Is it Grandma? Grandpa?" Logically, it had to be the elders in the family.

"No, no."

"Is it one of my sisters?" My hands began to shake as my mind wrestled against that possibility.

"Yes," she fairly whispered.

"Oh, God, Mom, who?" my voice rose hysterically.

"Beth."

"What happened to Beth?"

"No. Not Beth."

"Ken?" I asked.

"No, no."

My heart pounded as I uttered the names of my two nephews.

"Nick?"

"Alex?"

A scream rose in my chest. "No, Mom! Don't say it, Momma. Don't tell me. Please don't tell me."

My mother's voice filled my head. "Noah's been shot—"

It wasn't possible. Baby Noah was only three months old. Babies don't get shot.

"—in the head," she whispered.

Then I did scream. I dropped the phone and ran hysterically out the door of the apartment.

My husband picked up the line. The rest blurred together in rushed plans for flights and for staff and friends to operate my store. When we landed in Virginia, my brother-in-law, Vaughn, my oldest sister Pat's husband, met us at the airport. He had rushed to Virginia from North Carolina. I couldn't think of anything but my sister, my heart.

Beth's husband, Ken, had been wounded, too. His hand had been shattered when the bullet passed through it before slamming into Noah's head, his tiny, infant head. It entered below his eye and exited behind his ear. Miraculously, he survived. There were still two little boys at home who were confused and scared, surrounded by every face except the three they loved best: Mommy, Daddy, and Noah. I took care of them while my mother and brother-in-law shuttled Beth between hospitals. Finally, they brought Beth home for some sleep. She had been awake for nearly two days.

When Beth entered the house, I grabbed her in a hug. I sobbed. Beth didn't cry, but she fell into the embrace. I hadn't seen her in three years, and this was the worst possible way to reunite. I started to babble about all the things the boys and I had done during the long day.

She looked weary and lethargic. My mom signaled to get her upstairs, and I started to guide her toward the stairway. Beth stopped at the laundry room door. She struggled to say something but only a puff of air escaped her mouth.

"I'll get it later," I said, trying to reassure her that whatever chore had caught her attention would get done. She just stared until I finally saw what she was looking at: a soaking pan sitting on top of the washer.

Vaughn swept past Beth, muttering, "Oh, God."

The pale pink water from the pan splashed at our feet as he carried it away, and I realized it contained a small baby sleeper. I looked helplessly at Beth and caught her as she began to faint.

We managed to get her upstairs, and Mom and I got her ready for bed. I kept talking to her, knowing that when we were little girls, the sound of a voice could keep away her worst night terrors. Finally, I lay down beside her and took her hand. I wanted so badly for us to be eleven and twelve years old again.

Beth's body began to shake, and I turned so that I could hold her while she sobbed. But when I was facing her, I saw she was laughing.

"What?" I couldn't stop my own giggles from bubbling up to my throat.

She lay with her eyes tightly shut, laughing soundlessly. Finally, she managed to gasp, "I think if

I open my eyes and look at you, you will be wearing pink sponge rollers."

We began to laugh hysterically.

Our mother, hearing the commotion, added to the time-warp feeling by admonishing, "Girls, be quiet and go to sleep."

We both screeched with laughter.

Beth sat upright and sputtered, "I think I'm going to throw up."

She bolted for the bathroom, and I ran after her and held her as the heaves finally gave way to great, gulping sobs. We sat on the floor of the bathroom rocking and crying, as she asked over and over, "What am I going to do? What am I going to do?"

Our mother came in and joined us on the floor, rubbing our backs and saying, "Breathe, just breathe."

And so we did. We got up every morning and we breathed. So did our Noah Michael. Each day he breathed, and with each breath he grew stronger, and he grew into a wonderful, handsome, kind-hearted young man. He graduates from high school this year. And I will be there at his graduation, standing next to my sister, holding her hand, celebrating their victory, reminding her to breathe.

—Amy Williams

# Ah, Fruitcake!

I stood at the kitchen counter chopping pecans while my sister rifled through the lower cabinets between my legs in search of her industrial-sized baking sheets.

"Oh, this will be fun," she chattered, "baking our Thanksgiving fruitcake cookies together for the first time in years."

I spread my legs a little wider and looked down at her. "What are you talking about? I hate fruitcake."

If I had been a man I would have been castrated with one sharp blow. Her head came up so fast and with such force I barely had time to step back and out of the way. Her mouth gaped and her hands agitated the air from her position on the floor.

"Hush your mouth. Baking fruitcake cookies is a family tradition. We will do it and we will do it with the respect our foremothers set down for us many years ago."

I couldn't respond for a few moments. Finally, I said, "What planet are you from? I've never made fruit-cake cookies. We made cocoon wedding cookies, Santa-shaped sugar cookies, and Daddy's favorite, oatmeal with red and green M&Ms. But Mother never baked cookies with disgusting lumps of candied fruit."

Sissie's palm caught her scream. She bowed to the ground, almost weeping, like a female Dalai Lama doing penance for a horrible sin.

"Mother failed you, pure and simple," she managed to gasp. "I got married too young and left you to be raised by a menopausal wreck. She had me as a child and you as an old hag."

"What are you talking about?"

"You are my little sister and you know nothing about cookie tradition. What else did she fail to teach you? Do you have good dental hygiene? Do you have a clue how to bake bread? How many pickles do you put up each year? Did you breast-feed Mary Kate or was she a bottle baby? Oh, Lord, I think I might fall out right here."

"I turned out just fine, I'll have you know. But I don't know who you are talking about. The only pickles Mother ever put up were Claussen's. She got them from Kroger and put them up on the middle shelf in the refrigerator door. Wonder bread contributed to these hips, and Mary Kate did beautifully on Enfamil, thank you very much."

I then worried she might actually faint. The parenthesis around her mouth turned chalky and her eyes began to swim. I extended my hand and helped her up as she described family recipes and experiences I had never known. Was she delusional? Was she having a breakdown? I led her over to the kitchen table.

"It's okay," I said, patting her hand. "I'd love to learn how to make fruitcake cookies. You can teach me how."

She looked into my face, studying my newly arrived crow's feet as if she had never seen me before.

"Corn bread, you certainly know how to make corn bread."

"Jiffy muffin mix," I whispered, feeling inadequate.

"Pound cake. Tell me you know how to make pound cake."

"Duncan Hines."

"Spaghetti sauce?" Her eyes started to tear.

"Prego Traditional. It's good, honest."

"Oh, Lordy. I'll have to start from scratch." Her head lolled against the back of her chair, rolling back and forth like a pendulum of regret. Then she sat up straight as a wooden spoon and grabbed my shoulders so I could not escape. "You will learn the traditions of our heritage if I have to hold remedial classes from a nursing home."

Realizing I was dealing with a sister possessed and

that it would not be advantageous to put up a fuss, I nodded demurely and resumed my position at the counter with the other nuts. Sissie dug out the eight pounds of multicolored candied fruit that she'd stored since ought-one, refluffed herself, and took on her culinary duty with gusto. She instructed me on the proper way to chop our six cups of pecans. I was doing it wrong, of course.

"How many cookies are we making here?" I asked.

"Enough to feed the troops at Shiloh and every living friend and relative our family has claimed since I was born, except for Uncle Fred on Daddy's side, of course. Bill Ennis takes a dozen to his momma's grave instead of flowers each year. People are depending on us, so start chopping."

"And people really eat these things?"

I ducked as her hand whizzed past my head.

Then she explained how to ensure that our cookies had just the right amount of liquor to make them tasty but not so much that anyone would get soused.

"Liquor?" I said, perking up. With a shot or two of a decent libation I might survive this night without committing murder or hara-kiri.

"Apricot brandy," she replied with a dignified nod.

Not my favorite, but at that point I would've taken anything I could get. At first she refused the offer of a sip, but before long we were both chugging the stuff. Soon, we erupted into giggles and almost wet our pants.

When we recovered, I said, "I wish Mother had taught me these things. Maybe I would like fruitcake cookies if I had been introduced to them early on."

"Oh, you will like fruitcake cookies before this night is through," she reassured me. "If only I had Mother's recipe box, I could teach you everything you ever wanted to know about our culinary heritage. I wonder whatever happened to it?"

"You mean that old, green tin box?" I asked.

"That's the one."

Our eyes met. She knew what I was about to say, and it was everything she could do to keep from exploding into squeals before I got the words out.

"It's in my kitchen, in the cabinet over my stove."

The next thing she saw was my backside. Since I lived just down the street, I was back in record time, panting and holding the green box with all the reverence of the Holy Grail. I let her do the honors of lifting the lid. We gazed at the crumpled papers and note cards nestled within it as if we were looking into the womb of the Holy of Holies. Sissie fingered the edges of our mother's treasures and paused reverently before grasping one piece between her finger and thumb. She gave a tug.

*Mary Horst's (that's our mother)*
*Fresh Coconut Cake*

We both *aah'ed* and tears welled up. I removed the next jewel.

*Aunt Bill's Fresh Apple Cake*

We took turns ushering each recipe out of its tomb with all the fanfare we could muster without falling apart, blinking convulsively to clear the watershed flowing from our eyes.

*Aunt Willard's Angel Biscuits*
*Company Peas*
*Francis Stovall's to-Die-for Cheese Cake*
*Paula Ennis' Cranberry Orange Salad*
*Eggs a la King (no one claimed it)*
*Granny's Homemade Peach Ice Cream*

For some recipes, Sissie would recite a memory to go with it. As we took turns reading each title aloud in a kind of litany to our lineage, we could taste and smell each delicacy—and we could feel our mother right there with us, sitting across the kitchen table, smiling at the sisters she'd raised so differently, yet so closely.

By the time we had emptied our green memory tin, it was four o'clock in the morning, we had sobered up, and twenty-four dozen fruitcake cookies had been baked, cooled, and tinned. Most important, we had revived a family tradition that will last for generations to come.

Now, the week before Thanksgiving every year, we bake fruitcake cookies with my daughter—just like Sissie did in her youth. We always clear a place at the kitchen table for Mother to sit and listen in.

I didn't miss out on anything growing up, thanks to a sister who keeps our mother's legacy alive and well—and who loves me enough to teach me how to make cookies I despise.

—*Julia Horst Schuster*

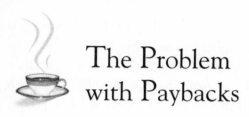

# The Problem with Paybacks

I grew up in an almost happy home. But there was Beth. I don't remember exactly when I realized she was a problem. I suspect it was shortly after she learned to talk, since words were usually her weapon of choice. I do know that the provocation peppers my earliest memories of her and that she became better at pestering me as time progressed. Having Beth for a sister was like having a cocklebur perpetually in my sock.

Beth seemed to live a charmed life. Fearless of new situations and new people, she brought out the green-eyed monster in me, the big sister, who cowered at both. In those days, rural pastors like our father moved every three or four years. By the time I was feeling comfortable in a new community, we'd move again.

Beth would tell you she, too, grew up in an almost happy home. But there was Virginia Ann.

~ 127 ~

Beth also frequently turned into the green-eyed monster, but for different reasons. Whereas I loved books and school and brought home grades that reaped high praise from Mama and Daddy, Beth wasn't all that interested in school and her grades were satisfactory but not stellar. She noticed the difference in our parents' approval.

As if that were not enough, I was often put in charge of my siblings. Because Daddy had eye problems, Mama had to drive him wherever he needed to go, and there were many visits to parishioners, conferences with other pastors, and speaking engagements. Mama appointed me supervisor of Beth and my other two sisters while our parents were away from home. Though my other younger sisters didn't mind and were usually cooperative, Beth didn't see the two-year age difference between us as being sufficient reason for me to be "the boss of" her. Of course, even Beth knew she had to do what I said while Mama and Daddy were gone. But she resented me for it and saw me as an overbearing autocrat who had no business telling her what to do.

She couldn't see the flip side of that coin: that Mama and Daddy held me accountable for whatever happened in their absence. And I resented Beth for making my job harder and for not recognizing that my responsibility was more of a burden than a privilege. I would gladly have traded my dependability for her free spirit.

A life pattern emerged that left both of us with hard feelings and little appreciation for the other. Though Beth did not dare retaliate against my authority while our parents were away, she found ways to get even when they were home. She'd watch for my touchy subjects, and there were many, then throw verbal jabs aimed right at them, irritating me until I lost my temper. It usually didn't take long. Physically bigger and stronger than she was, I would strike out.

Immediately, she would call, "Mama, Virginia Ann hit me!"

Of course, I had, and I paid the price. Beth, of course, never mentioned what she had said to pick the fight. And I, self-righteously, said nothing . . . and seethed.

Eventually, I figured out Beth's strategy and decided to get my revenge with words rather than fists. To my frustration, I soon discovered that Beth had far fewer touchy subjects than I did and that I was more of a loose thread than a cocklebur in her sock. Beth continued to work me into a smoldering fury with her verbal assaults, and I, determined to give her back some of her own medicine, continued to badger and belittle her. Yet, nothing I said or did seemed to faze her. Her feelings were obviously not as sensitive as mine. But I was determined to break through that thick skin, and I watched for an opportunity. I found it shortly before Christmas.

Mama took the four of us girls to the county seat to go Christmas shopping. Mama gave us each a small amount of money to buy presents for each other. We didn't have much to spend, so our choices were limited to whatever we could find in the dime store where Mama took us to shop. To complicate things for the other girls, I had reached the stage in adolescence where toys held little pleasure for me.

After we girls finished shopping, Mama sent us to the car to wait while she made her purchases. I glanced at the paper bags clutched in Beth's hands and figured out from their shape that she had bought Play-Doh for each of us.

"I know what's in there," I baited her.

She bit at my taunt and said, "No, you don't."

"Yes, I do. It's Play-Doh."

"Is not."

"Is too."

"You don't know," she said.

But I knew she was covering up—and I knew my moment of victory had arrived.

"Well," I said smugly, "I'm glad, because I hate Play-Doh. It's so childish."

I saw her shrink, but I continued my diatribe about the stupidity of Play-Doh until she was in tears.

I can still see her eyes. I had never seen that look before. I also had never seen her cry like that. It brought me no pleasure. When Mama got to the car, she comforted Beth and then took her back into the store to help her get another present that was more appropriate for my age. I don't remember what it was.

During the ten-mile drive home that day, I puzzled over the situation. Why did Beth get such pleasure from hurting my feelings when I got none from hurting hers? How could I take back what I had said? I could not. The damage had been done.

Beth and I grew up and became friends as well as sisters. Eventually we came to understand that the problem we'd had with each other as children came from life circumstances that were nobody's fault. Other life circumstances—marriage, children close to the same age, husbands whose jobs kept us on the move every few years—brought us closer together as adults. Today, when life gives either of us a bad turn or a good one, we are likely to call the other to talk about it.

Through the years the Christmas episode nagged at the back of my mind. I finally worked up the courage to talk with Beth about it a few years ago. She didn't remember it. Yet, I recall it all vividly, as if it were yesterday—the town square and the street corner where the dime store used to stand, its narrow aisles and the smell of cashews roasting in the corner, sitting in Mama's Ford station wagon, seeing the tell-tale lumps in the paper bags, and making my sister cry.

I learned two lessons from Beth: one on that day of Christmas shopping long ago, the other more recently during a sister talkathon that went on hours after we should have been asleep. She didn't set out to teach me either. First, she showed me that vengeance brings pain, not pleasure—that in deliberately hurting someone else, you also hurt yourself. Late at night years later, she showed me that peace comes to those who forgive and forget and never to those who hold on to hurt and regret.

—Virginia McGee Butler

# The Worst Babysitter in the Whole World

I charged down the stairs and rounded the corner into the hallway. When I caught sight of my mother, I stopped dead in my tracks. She was wearing earrings and a nice dress.

"Are you going out tonight?" I asked.

"Yes."

My heart dropped. "Do you have to?"

"Yes, I do, as a matter of fact. Don't worry. Rebecca will be here to take care of you."

That was the whole problem. My older sister, Rebecca, was the worst babysitter in the world. She would assign us younger kids the chores we had to do, and then she would ascend the stairs to her room, where she'd sit and read beauty magazines, gaze at her Beatles posters, try on makeup, and coordinate the clothes in her closet. We'd slave away at our respective tasks, listening for her feet on the stairs.

Inevitably, she'd descend to the main floor of our house to check on our progress. She'd always find fault with what we'd done. I don't remember a single time when she said, "You did a good job. Now, let's have some ice cream." In fact, I have a vivid mental picture of her standing in the dining room, her hands resting on her hips while she swept one bare foot across the floor in front of her in half circles.

"I feel crumbs," she'd say. "Sweep it again."

Well, on this particular night, when Rebecca's polished toenails led her up to her room like a princess ascending to her tower, something inside me snapped. I called my younger siblings into a huddle.

"It's not fair that she makes us do all the work and she doesn't have to do any," I said.

Greg and Loraine looked up at me with wide eyes. "Yeah," they agreed.

"Let's just do half of our jobs and leave the other half for Rebecca," I said.

"What if she doesn't do it?" Greg asked.

"We'll hide, and then when Mom gets home, we'll tell her that we did our parts and Rebecca has to do the rest."

"Yeah!"

So we set to our tasks with renewed energy. We cleared half the supper dishes from the table, washed exactly half the dishes (we even counted them), and stopped the broom halfway across the kitchen floor.

When everything was done by halves, we decided on our hiding places. Greg and Loraine were intrigued with the idea of hiding under the kitchen sink. It looked like they'd both fit—that is, after we'd cleared out the cleaners, soap bottles, buckets, sponges, and rubber gloves. They crawled inside, and I handed them a flashlight and shut the door. I was making my way toward my own hiding place when I heard the royal feet descending the staircase. I knew I wouldn't make it. I looked around in panic.

Just then, Greg popped open the cupboard door. "Shirley, we need new batteries."

"Shhhh!" I warned.

"Here she comes," Loraine warned.

I ducked down beside the piano just in time. Rebecca strode through the living room, right on past me, and into the kitchen.

"What do you think you're doing?" Rebecca demanded.

Greg and Loraine fell silent. I got up from my crouch and stood erect. Heart pounding, I faced my older sister.

"It's not fair that you make us do everything," I said. "We think you should have to do some of the work, too."

Rebecca stared at me. "You all just made more work for yourselves." She pointed imperiously to the pile of cleaning supplies on the kitchen floor. "Put everything back where it was. And finish your jobs. Right now."

Her demeanor reminded me of the time she'd made me eat a canned tamale, even though I told her I hated canned tamales. As soon as I'd choked down the last bite, I ran for the bathroom and threw up. Once again, I did as she told, and we put everything back under the sink and finished our chores, too.

Not long after the night of our failed rebellion, our mother had a baby girl named Carolyn. She had blond hair, blue eyes, and Down's syndrome.

I didn't even know what Down's syndrome was. I went around telling people that my baby sister was retarded. I said it with the same enthusiasm as I used when relaying that she had blond hair and blue eyes . . . until my father overheard me giving someone the news.

"Shirley, that's enough." His clipped voice let me know I had done something wrong, though I couldn't for the life of me figure out what it was. I was truly confused.

Rebecca knew what Down's syndrome was, and having a retarded sister was not something a young teenage girl would normally be proud of. Rebecca told me later that she dreaded going to sleep at night because of the nightmares that plagued her. In those horrible, unwanted dreams, her adolescent turmoil vented itself in terrifying scenarios in which she killed her baby sister. She'd wake up shaking, her heart pounding so hard it hurt, her pillow wet with tears.

In desperation, Rebecca turned to prayer for help in overcoming her awful nighttime phantoms. She began spending more time with Carolyn. She'd hold her while watching television. She offered to change Carolyn's diaper, and when she did, she would talk to the baby and tickle her feet, coaxing smiles from her round, slant-eyed face. Rebecca even bathed Carolyn, supporting her small, limp body in the bathtub.

"Kick, kick, kick!" Rebecca said, encouraging Carolyn to move her little limbs through the warm water.

Rebecca took Carolyn for walks and pointed out the sights. She got down on her hands and knees to help Carolyn learn to crawl, and ultimately, she taught her to walk. Rebecca's nightmares soon stopped, but that wasn't the only good thing to come out of her experience. I almost couldn't believe it when she invited me to go to a party with her. I am three years younger than Rebecca, and at the time, that was just the right age difference to make most older sisters not want to be caught dead hanging around with their kid sister.

At the party, we had refreshments and played games like Who Stole the Cookies from the Cookie Jar? When Rebecca said, "Shirley stole the cookies from the cookie jar," my heart leapt in amazement.

Not only had she wanted me along, but she also included me in the game.

After that, Rebecca invited me to dance practice with her friends, let me borrow her clothes, and spent hours helping me with a musical number for a contest. Then, miracle of miracles, Rebecca asked me to stay up with her when she was babysitting late for our parents. We sat together on the couch, snuggled together under an afghan, eating chocolate cream pie and watching an old movie on television. That's when the worst babysitter in the world magically turned into the best big sister a girl could have.

—*Shirley Anderson Bahlmann*

# Hand in Hand

Peggy didn't have a clue about what was in store for her when Carroll drove up to the Our Lady of the Lake Hospital admissions door. A gray fog hung over the small lake behind the low building, and the clangs of tugs and barges moving swiftly down the Mississippi River echoed just beyond the nearby levy.

Carroll carefully helped his wife to the curb and patted her with gentle assurance. "I'll be right back as soon as I park the car. You just wait right inside the door for me, okay? I love you."

"Okay," Peggy mumbled as she waddled into the lobby. Even though it was only a little after 7:00 A.M., the Southern September heat and humidity were already pressing down on her that morning in 1959. The black-and-white-checked A-line maternity blouse jutted out over the unflattering straight black skirt, making her massive belly seem even bigger. As Peggy fanned herself with an old magazine, Carroll was spit out by the revolving doors into the waiting room. He was combing his hair into the customary ducktail, his eyes frantically searching the interior. As soon as he saw his beautiful young wife, he relaxed.

Many hours later, a nurse searched for the father-to-be. He heard the starched and ironed fabric of her uniform approaching and bolted awake. The excitement of the previous night and worry over his wife's going into labor six weeks shy of her official due date had sapped him.

"Mr. DiBon—, DeeBen—, DieBenDe—?" she questioned.

"Yes, I'm Carroll DiBenedetto," he answered.

"I have some blessed news for you. Your healthy daughter was just born. She and Peggy are doing just fine."

"Oh, my. Thank you." His Adam's apple pumped furiously as he fought back happy tears.

"And she was joined by your other daughter two minutes later."

"Another daughter? Two girls? Twins? Really?" the young father sputtered.

"Yes, twins. I'll bring you to see all three of your girls shortly." The nurse smiled.

Peggy and Carroll named the older twin Alaine and the younger twin Angie. The premature sisters held hands while they slept, nestled together in the same bassinet, and they grew into happy, healthy toddlers who spoke their own private language.

On July 14, 1984, twin brides stood together looking out of a fifteenth-story building. The sunset painted a heavenly mural reflecting off the Mississippi River flowing past the now-closed Lady of the Lake Hospital. The bold reds, yellows, and tangerines cast from the departing sun dappled their clasped hands. They hugged each other as their grooms joined them near the front of the seated crowd.

Peggy and Carroll watched from the first row of chairs with much the same look of joy, exhaustion, and amazement that they'd worn twenty-five years earlier. Their girls, flanked by twelve bridesmaids, groomsmen, and their new sons-in-law, looked beautiful in their wedding gowns. Alaine and Angie, like their dresses, were so different, yet so much alike. The lump in Carroll's throat rippled again as he wiped his misty eyes and gave his twin daughters away to a new life of their own.

Six years later, Alaine pushed Angie's wheelchair through the hospital's electronically opened doors. Both wore the exact same outfit: cotton pastel overalls with a bold teal T-shirt underneath. The first attendant to see them fled in the opposite direction, muttering, "No, sir, no sir . . . pregnant twins . . . I can't handle that." Giggling, the two expectant moms joined hands.

Six days later, they returned to the hospital. This time, Angie wheeled in Alaine. They waved cheerily to the same attendant and went to find a nurse. Within less than a week, they had each given birth to sons—in the same delivery room, with the same shift of doctors and nurses. The ensuing confusion and fun was only a small part of their parallel life experience.

Their sons, born so near together, grew up more like brothers than cousins. As the years passed, the twin sisters, now women with families of their own, remained as close as ever. Their successes, joys, and adventures were multiplied by sharing. Likewise, their losses, hurts, and sorrows were halved. Every year, a few days before their actual birth date, they celebrated their shared birthday together with their parents, Peggy and Carroll.

After ringing in their fortieth year with the traditional birthday meal of hotdogs and French fries cooked by Peggy, the talk naturally turned to the many events and escapades of their lives.

"Remember the time we fooled our dates?"

"Remember the boyfriend who hated sharing you with me, so y'all broke up?"

"I remember when you girls were only two and got the notion to go visit our neighbors. While I was on the phone you lifted each other up to unlatch the screen door and ran off down the street in your birthday suits."

For a good long while, parents and daughters sat around the worn wooden table, laughing and crying together as they reminisced. Recalling all the good twin times was one of the best things about sharing a birthday. Soon two gifts appeared, wrapped in the same dark purple, flowered wallpaper that Peggy had used for twenty years.

They laughed and teased about what Peggy would do if the roll of paper ever ran out, because surely it had been discontinued long ago.

"She'll just go back to using the funny pages from the Sunday paper," the twins said in stereophonic glee.

Carroll and Peggy gave each daughter a large box, inside which were nested four or five smaller boxes in gradually descending size, all wrapped in the floral wallpaper. This family custom was designed to draw out the agony and anticipation for the recipient, who had to paw through layers of tissue and wrapped boxes to find the gift.

When Angie finally got to her last box, she found three envelopes inside. The first held a funny card about getting older but not necessarily wiser. The second envelope contained the description of a beautiful resort in Jackson Hole, Wyoming, along with a reservation confirmation letter for an upcoming weekend. With shaking hands, she opened the third one to find a confirmation letter for a retreat conference and a round-trip airline ticket.

Mascara-filled tears dripped onto Angie's shirt. She couldn't believe she was actually going to the retreat she'd been dreaming of for months. Only her parents and twin sister had known how much she needed to get away and recharge her spiritual batteries in a quiet setting. When her mind could focus again, she looked over at her twin's gift: a beautiful Art Deco tea set. Her sister was smiling happily, apparently not noticing the disparity in the two gifts. Knowing their parents would never treat them differently, she looked from face to face for a clue, and it suddenly dawned on her what had happened.

"You asked Mother and Daddy not to give you a gift and to do this for me, didn't you?" she asked Alaine.

Her twin, eyes glistening with tears and mischief, nodded and made the zip-your-lip motion of their childhood language. The sign meant no talking was allowed or needed, that all was understood between them. Fresh tears sprang to their eyes as they grabbed each other's hand.

As thrilled as Angie was to be going on the trip, she couldn't help but feel a little sad, too. No adventure or endeavor could be complete without her twin there beside her. Taking photographs and keeping a trip journal to share when she returned couldn't compare with sharing the experience together.

Weeks passed and the day of departure arrived. Carroll and Peggy drove their daughter to the airport, and naturally, Alaine tagged along. Parents and daughters ate sandwiches in an airport café and watched travelers come and go until the flight was called. Holding hands, the twins walked to the departure gate with their parents. The sisters stood side by side, hands clenched tightly together, until all the other passengers had boarded and the final boarding call was announced. Angie broke away to hug her parents goodbye. Trying hard not to cry, she hugged her sister, and then, before turning to leave, she grasped her twin's hand for one last hard squeeze.

"Hey, wait! Here's the ticket," Alaine called after her twin, pulling a white envelope out of her purse and waving it in the air.

Angie paused in confusion, glancing at her own purse. "No, I have my ticket right here," she said, pulling the boarding pass and return ticket from the pocket of her bag.

"I didn't say 'your' ticket, silly. I said 'the' ticket . . . *my* ticket!"

The sisters dropped their bags and began doing their squealing-hugging-hopping-in-a-circle dance, as Angie screamed, "You're coming with me! You're coming with me!" at the top of her lungs. Only when they'd stopped their crazy motions did they notice the gawking passersby and the crowd that had gathered and were now clapping and laughing.

After thanking their parents and giving them another quick hug, the twins clasped hands and skipped to the plane, giggling all the way. They might have looked more like four-year-olds than forty-year-olds, but they didn't care. They were off for a few glorious days of rest, relaxation, and solitude—together, of course.

—*Angie Ledbetter*

# Finding Tigers, Losing Janet

Today I begin my journey in India. I sit in a small hotel room in Delhi. The windows are tightly shut, though it is a blistering 90 degrees outside. The air pollution is so intense it is not safe to venture outdoors.

I meditate. Breathe in, breathe out. I feel the breathing of my sister, Janet, halfway across the world, as she struggles to survive. My sister and I have always loved cats. For her, cats represent the highest qualities embodied on Earth: equanimity, independence, humor, and mystery. For me, cats have made being a human more fun. To be in the presence of one of the most threatened and beautiful large cats on the planet is a dream I have had my whole life. I am now in India to see the Bengal tiger.

As I sit, I see Janet curled up on her couch: eyes, now so prominent in a gaunt face, bones revealed beneath skin stretched thin over a constant grimace of pain. The cancer found originally in her breast many years ago now eats away at her liver and cripples her spine. She stares into the woods of oak and elm surrounding her house near Chesapeake Bay, ever seeking the birds she has taught me to love. Occasionally she lifts her heavy Zeiss binoculars to pick out an old friend migrating south over the nearby pond. These binoculars have been from Venezuela to Botswana. Janet was always on a search for a new bird to add to her life list, the record of all the birds she has observed. She has told me she wants me to have these glasses when she can no longer lift them to her eyes.

In my backpack is a bird list describing what I am likely to see in the national parks I will be visiting in India. When Janet and I pored over this list together, I watched the longing build in her face.

"I'd love to be going with you," she said. "This great white ibis I have always wanted to see."

I wonder this morning how I could have left her behind. But she has made it clear she'll never forgive me if I give up this trip.

The next day at dawn, I gather with other tiger seekers. I carefully pick the guide who I feel might be luckier in the search and jump into his jeep. Our Indian naturalist guide, Dharmendra, is an expert tracker of the tiger. After several hours in the jungle, we meet up with another jeep. The two drivers speak excitedly, gesticulating wildly, and though I don't understand Urdu, it is clear the other jeep occupants have seen a tiger. Their guide explains they have been tracking a female tiger for several hours and observed her kill a small chital deer. When she dragged her fallen prey into thick grasses, they lost sight of her, just an hour earlier. Now they feel she will soon be ready to come out of her eating and napping spot and go to the nearby lake for a drink. She will need to cross a road near where we are. We careen toward the spot where she is most likely to emerge.

There she is, lying on her belly, facing the road, most of her body visible on the edge of the grass. Each tiger has a different pattern of stripes, and hers is particularly elegant. She is gently washing her face, blood from her kill still on the sides of her mouth. She is far larger than I had anticipated. Her eyes are yellow, and she looks directly at us.

Tears well up in my eyes, as I feel how far I have traveled and how acutely I miss the sister I have left behind in order to be with this tiger at this moment. But my grief is compounded by another loss, knowing the Bengal tiger is quickly moving toward extinction. I am overwhelmed, both with gratitude for the privilege of witnessing this cat and with sorrow in knowing it will undoubtedly be my last opportunity to be in the presence of this great beast. As this tiger's home is being polluted and destroyed by a rising Indian population, so is Janet's body. Her spirit, her passion for cats and birds, will soon no longer have a physical asylum.

She and I are eight years apart in age, and we have only become close in the last few years. The suffering she has had to endure in her early forties, as her body has tried, and finally failed, to fend off the cancer has horrified me. Just as she and I were beginning to develop a friendship, cemented by our mutual love of wildlife, I began to lose her.

As we pull away to leave the tigress in peace, I look one last time at her. She symbolizes for me all the best qualities of womanhood: wildness, sensuality, mystery, and wisdom. She lies there, replete with food she has caught and killed. Her belly, full and warm from digestion, cools on the wet sand of the marsh. The high grasses she claims as home gently stroke her fur. She reminds me of the grace of my own body when I have danced or played soccer. In my last glimpse of her, I mentally carry Janet to this Indian swamp and bring her to this tigress. Above, in an old tree snag, sits a huge white ibis, the bird so dear to my sister. As he gazes down at the tiger and the circle of humans nearby, I know Janet is here with me. I say goodbye. In the dwindling light, we drive recklessly toward the entrance of the park, obeying the rule that all vehicles must leave by dusk.

Three months later I am sitting with my sister on

her couch. She has just celebrated her forty-sixth birthday. Her face is even gaunter, her belly distended. Her oncologist has taken her off all treatments, and she is now home facing the last few weeks of her life. We have been going through old photographs and telling more secrets about their stories. I have been helping her choose which friends and family members will receive her various favorite possessions. She continues through these necessary jobs with good humor. The pain pills keep her spirits up.

Outside it is a drizzly spring day. The daffodils shoot their golden heads out of oak leaf piles below her deck. We stare together quietly at the brilliant red male cardinal feasting on sunflower seeds at the birdfeeder outside the plate glass door. The list of birds I saw in India lies on the cushions between us. She listens with keen interest to the tantalizing names and descriptions of new birds for her: alexandrine parakeet, stork-billed kingfisher, Indian white-backed vulture, crimson-breasted barbet. She would have added them to her life list had she gone to India with me.

I have always been a little suspicious of birders' life lists. Had Janet's continuing effort to find and log new birds been her fight to stave off death? I have not been able to understand the need to identify more and more species. For me, simply spotting a red-capped manakin in the thick greenery of a Costa Rican rainforest was an experience of the highest order. It would never have occurred to me to write down his name on a list. As I have observed over the years my sister's enthusiasm to accumulate birds on her life list, I have learned that knowledge of an animal is another expression of love for it. My sister's recording of these birds increased my awareness of their habitat and their needs for water and food along their flight paths, whether from Central America to the tip of Alaska or from South Africa along the Indian coast into central Europe. The birds' endurance and spirit to survive is the gift my sister has given me.

Janet sits on her couch, grimacing every few minutes as the pain increases. Gus, her four-year-old, carrot-headed neighbor sits with a few toys on the floor near her. They have adored each other his entire life. He continues to visit her daily. Though he seems calm and accepting that they play less now than he is accustomed to, she is clearly frustrated at not being able to reach out and pull him onto her lap.

Her voice has become like a dry piece of paper crackling. "Anne, please go over to that basket with my birding stuff, next to the glass door. Bring me my Zeiss binoculars."

I retrieve the heavy old glasses and hand them to her. She fondles them gently. I remember her in the Yucatan, bathing in the sun. Then, her spirit filled her rotund, voluptuous body. After birding at dawn, she enjoyed the rising heat, these binoculars resting lightly on her chest—one real breast and one manu-factured, following her mastectomy.

Now I can see in her glazed look that she is returning to resplendent quetzals in the Costa Rican mountain cloud forests, violaceous trogons on the Caribbean coasts, great horned owls in the high deserts of south-eastern Arizona, Anna's hummingbirds in her own back-yard. She hands me the glasses, her second pair of eyes.

"I won't need these anymore. I want you to have them now."

Gus watches me as I struggle not to scream with shock at losing my only sister. To use these glasses spotting birds without her feels unbearably lonely.

I struggle to look at my little sister through a haze of tears. She dozes, her dear cat, Sasha, spread over her dis-tended stomach. Walking silently out onto her deck, I gaze through her binoculars to the pond a few hundred yards away. Their magnification is precise. It is looking through her eyes. The far world becomes intimate. My sister will not visit this pond again. In a few minutes I must leave to return to my home in Seattle, 3,000 miles away. This is the last time I will ever see her face.

I awaken her and take her in my arms. She looks up at me, drowsy and scared. Her eyes fill with tears and search mine for some relief. Holding back my own tears, I silently hold her. Neither of us can face this goodbye, and we pull away, fingers still entwined. Turning my back on my sister to walk out her front door feels impossible.

She can barely say, "Goodbye."

These are the last words I will hear her speak. She looks, suddenly, terribly young. I remember a photo of the two of us. I am nine and she only one, newly walking. Emerging from a swimming pool, we are both wet. Holding hands, we smile shyly at the camera in our matching yellow rose-printed bathing suits. Her intense curiosity about the world shines through enormous blue eyes. Leaning against me, her soft tummy curves into my leg, her curly blond head rests on my waist. I have always protected her, until now.

Embracing her tiny wasted body for the last time, through my tears, I whisper, "I love you, Janet."

Clutching my sister's heavy binoculars to my chest, I walk out the front door of her home for the last time.

At Janet's wake a few weeks later, her many friends are gathered on the deck outside her house. We are quiet as the raucous calls of jays and cardinals fill the void. Gus is talking to his mother.

She says, "Gus, when you talk to the angels at night before going to bed, you can now say hello to Janet, because she is with them."

Gus grows unusually silent for a moment. His green eyes cloud, and then he suddenly brightens. "No, Mom," he says. "Janet is not an angel. She is a butterfly tiger."

—Anne Brownson Mize

# Hair Care

My sister Jodie was the popular, good-looking sister; I was the nerdy, plain one. While she had a flair for fashion, I consistently made fashion blunders. Almost eight years younger than my stylish older sister, I never had a chance to catch up with her. But that didn't stop me from trying. She tried to help me, too, but I just didn't possess her fashion finesse. The hair was the hardest thing to compete with. Mine was a mousy brown; hers, a dazzling red. She never even dyed her hair; it was naturally the most amazing color—not carrot red or strawberry blond, but a deep, luxurious, almost burgundy red. It was the most outstanding of her many attractive features, and everyone—including Mom and Dad—constantly complimented her on her gorgeous hair.

The year I was seven, I was walking past her room one morning and spotted her sitting at her vanity with the scissors in her hand.

"Jo," I said. "Are you cutting off your hair?" I was sort of hoping she was.

"No," she laughed. "As if! I'm just going to cut a fringe."

"A fringe?"

"Yeah," she said. "Fringes are in now."

I sat and watched her wet her hair with water from a spray bottle, comb a section of it down over her forehead, and cut it in a straight line across her forehead.

"Wow," I said when she'd finished. "That looks good."

It did look good. It framed her perfectly oval face nicely, making her look even prettier.

Mom and Dad commented on how nice it looked over breakfast.

"Maybe I could get a fringe, too," I suggested.

Mom looked at me for a minute. "I don't know whether it would suit your face shape, darling."

"Why not? What's wrong with the shape of my face?"

"Nothing. You and your sister have different face shapes, that's all."

"It might look nice," Jodie interjected.

Mom looked at me again, creasing her brow.

"Hmmm, maybe," she said. But she didn't seem convinced.

I just shrugged and went back to eating my breakfast.

After breakfast Jodie went out to spend the day with her friends. I snuck up to her room and sat in front of her mirror, looking at myself hard, imagining myself with a fringe, thinking about what Jodie had said about fringes being in fashion now.

"I'll show them," I mumbled and picked up the scissors.

Copying exactly what Jodie had done, I cut myself a fringe. When I was done, I looked triumphantly at my new haircut in the mirror, but it didn't seem quite right. Somehow, my fringe didn't look as great as Jodie's did.

*I know,* I thought, *what I need is a fringe that goes all the way around, not just in front.*

I sprayed all of my hair, combed it down straight, and began to cut. I cut around as far as I could reach, trying to go in a straight line. I picked up the hand mirror and turned around to check out the back. It wasn't close to being straight. I took the scissors and tried again. This time it was too short at the back. I cut around the front and sides again to even it up. I looked at the back again, but it still wasn't straight. The left side was much higher than the right. I cut the left to straighten it up. An hour later, I looked in the mirror and realized there wasn't much else I could do. My hair now sat about an inch above my ears, and it wasn't even close to being straight all the way round. It went up and down in a zigzag shape. Realizing what I'd done, I began to panic. I ruffled it up to see if that would help. It didn't. I rewet it, combed it straight, and was about to go at it again when Mom walked in with Jodie's laundry.

"Oh, no," she gasped, dropping the laundry in the middle of the floor.

"What?" I said calmly, brushing my hair back like I was some kind of supermodel.

"What have you done?" she said.

"I gave myself a fringe like Jodie's. Better than Jodie's, actually, because mine goes all the way around," I said, turning my head to the side in a dramatic pose I'd seen in *Seventeen* magazine.

"Oh, no," she said again.

Mom sat down next to me and ruffled my hair, moving it this way and that.

"Oh, honey. What have you done?" she said again.

I started to cry. "I'm sorry. I just wanted to be pretty."

"Don't cry," Mom said. "It'll be all right. It'll grow back."

"Soon?" I asked.

I spent the rest of the day hiding in my room. I heard Jodie come home, and then I heard her talking with Mom. I guessed Mom was filling her in on my fringe fiasco. Then I heard a soft knock on my door and Jodie came in.

"Oh, no," she said, putting her hand to her mouth. Then she started to laugh.

"Don't laugh!" I wailed. "It's your fault, you know. I just wanted to be pretty like you."

"Sorry, I didn't mean to laugh. It's just . . ."

"Shut up," I said, burying my head in my pillow.

Jodie stayed for a few minutes longer, telling me not to worry about it and that it wasn't a big deal.

"What would you know?" I said from under my pillow. "You don't know what it's like to look like me. You're so pretty. Everything you do is so perfect."

Jodie got up and quietly left my room. I buried my head a little deeper into my pillow, feeling sorrier for myself than I ever had before. Twenty minutes later, I heard Jody come in again. I ignored her.

"Hey, Shell," she said. "Get your head out of there. I want to show you something."

"No," I mumbled.

"Come on, it won't take long."

"No," I said. "I'm never leaving this room ever. I don't want to be laughed at."

"Please, Shell, just pull your head out of there for a minute."

Finally, I relented and rolled over.

"Oh, no," I said when I saw her standing in the doorway, putting my hand to my mouth in shock.

"What have you done?"

Then she twirled around, patting her new zigzag hairdo like she was Marilyn Monroe.

"I call it 'the Zag,'" she said. "It's the latest fashion, you know."

"It looks terrible," I giggled.

"It's not so bad," she said, smiling. "In fact, I think it'll catch on. Before you know it, the Zag will be all the rage."

"You really think so?"

"Man, I hope so."

When I got on the school bus the next day, a bunch of the girls started laughing. Then Jodie stepped on behind me. As the girls watched Jodie stroll confidently down the aisle, they stopped laughing. I wouldn't go so far as to say they'd decided I was fashionable, but at least I was no longer a laughingstock.

The Zag never did catch on, but Jodie's and my hair did eventually grow out. I still think it was the most horrid hairstyle I've ever seen. But I've never had a hairdo that made me feel better about myself. Even now, every time I think of Jodie with the Zag, it makes me smile and it makes me feel pretty special to have a sister who'd do that for me.

—Shelley Ann Wake

# Three-Part Harmony

"My baby sister is going to be eighty!"

My sister Hannah, nine years my senior, is calling me from the nursing home where she lives in New Jersey. I live in Florida.

Hannah has never called me her baby sister, not to my face. Perhaps without being conscious of it, she has slipped back to that time almost eighty years ago when I was presented to her in swaddling clothes, all three pounds of me, and she was told, "This is your new baby sister."

Between us, in the middle, is Natalie, six years younger than Hannah, three years older than me. Our birth order defined our relationships. I was Hannah's toy; she loved to play with me and show me off. To Natalie, I was a kid sister, an annoyance at best. As the baby of the family I had a sense of entitlement. One day, because I was dawdling, Natalie left for high school before me. I seized the opportunity to rummage through her side of the closet and put on one of her outfits, a two-piece burgundy gabardine with leg-of-mutton sleeves—risky business, since we attended the same school. When our paths crossed later that day in a crowded corridor, Natalie's face said it all: *Just you wait, you little snot!* When we got home she chased me around the dining room table. Then my mother got into the act, chasing the two of us, swatting us with a dishtowel.

Natalie and I shared a bedroom: twin beds with blue and white tufted bedspreads, a walnut bureau that magically opened to become a desk, a matching vanity with a big round mirror, and a small upholstered vanity bench. In the dark before falling asleep, moving our hands every which way, we made shadow pictures on the wall, told ghost stories, giggled, whispered secrets, quarreled, called each other names. "Goon" was our favorite.

Whatever our differences, sooner or later they dissolved in song. We had good voices and ears for music. Natalie and I liked nothing better than to lie in bed and harmonize the songs we'd learned in school: "Sweet and Low," "All Through the Night," "Brahms' Lullaby." Usually, Natalie sang the melody and I did the harmony. If I didn't know the notes I made them up, fumbling around until they sounded right. Natalie was a perfectionist. One wrong note and she'd cry, "No!" We had to start all over again.

I thought of Natalie as a music nut. On Saturday afternoons when I couldn't wait to go to the movies with a girlfriend, Natalie, in her maroon robe, her chestnut hair in metal curlers that framed her soft, delicate face, sat glued to the radio listening to the Metropolitan Opera. If our mother happened to come into the room she would mumble something about "*kvitching.*" *Kvitching* could mean anything from the chirping of birds to the trilling of operatic voices.

As we grew older, my sisters and I progressed from "Sweet and Low" to "Joseph, Joseph" and "Rum and Coca Cola." We were better-looking than the Andrews sisters, but they had nothing to fear from us. At large family celebrations we were expected to perform, usually between courses, somewhere between the chicken soup and the rainbow sherbet. We rose and shot each other warning glances that said, *Don't you dare mess this up.* Our trademark song was "Sophisticated Swing." After a few *ahems* and false starts, we'd began with, "Honey, mascara your eyebrows and come with me." My favorite part was, "Mind, we must dance refined." I loved to stretch the first note for five beats, all the while fantasizing about dancing *un*refined.

Mostly, my sisters and I sang at home. We invented rhymes and parodies spontaneously. Once, when my mother was boiling a pot of rice, her standard remedy for diarrhea, she said, "It's binding," and the three of us immediately began singing, "Never try to bind me," one of those kitschy songs from the 1930s. Usually, my mother laughed, but there were times when she would look at us as if to say, *If the three of you had been kittens, I would have drowned you at birth.*

Whenever I think of that time, I remember the evening gowns that were part of Hannah's college wardrobe: the slinky gold satin with the halter top and plunging back, the ivory crepe with the red velvet spaghetti straps, the ankle-length black velvet evening wrap with the white fox collar. Was it real fox, or had it, as my mother was fond of saying, "only laid near a fox"? With her white crushed-velvet evening gloves reaching almost to her shoulders, her slender figure, green eyes, and long, wavy blond hair, Hannah turned heads. She was my role model. I knew I could never look like her, but I could smoke cigarettes like her, which I wasted no time in doing. At fourteen, I was a secret smoker.

Once a week or so my mother would take us to Sibley's Tea Room in downtown Rochester. We'd nibble nut bread and cream cheese finger sandwiches to the strains of "Welcome, Sweet Springtime" and other uplifting melodies played by three plain-faced elderly ladies: a cellist, a violinist, and a pianist. I thought then that they must have been at least a hundred years old, but for all I knew, they could have been in their thirties or younger.

On the eve of my wedding fifty-seven years ago, the memory of the tea room trio tickled Hannah's funny bone. Grabbing a handful of coat hangers, she gave two apiece to Natalie and me, then announced to assorted dinner guests, "Vee vill now play a little after-dinner musik." Seating ourselves in a circle, we hoisted our dresses, spread our knees apart, and using the hangers as cellos and bows, bellowed, "Oh Promise Me" and "Because."

I was the first to marry. The next day, after my wedding, which took place in our family home, as I was changing into my "going away" outfit, Hannah suddenly disappeared. We found her sobbing in the bathroom.

"It will never be the same!" she cried.

Absorbed in the excitement of my wedding day, I didn't feel the impact of her words at the time, didn't realize until many years later that she was weeping over the loss of her baby sister.

Hannah was right: It never was the same. It was better. The experiences of marriage, raising children, widowhood, and divorce have forged new bonds between us. The loss of our parents and the inevitable assaults of old age have taken their toll on us, but at the same time, have drawn us closer. In difficult times we have always reached for and been comforted by one another. Now, late in our lives, keenly aware of our mortality, we cling to each other, to our shared memories. Whatever rough edges there may have been in our relationships in our youth, the years have smoothed away.

No one else—not our husbands, our children, our closest friends—knows the entirety of us. We are the keepers of each other's youthful dreams, from child-hood to old womanhood. Across the miles we talk with one another, gently, with terms of endearment. Our conversations are filled with reminiscences: our parents, cousins, aunts, and uncles; family picnics at Genesee Valley Park, where I once brought home a frog, and when it died Hannah and Natalie con-ducted a funeral service; the cottage on Lake Ontario, with the wraparound porch where every evening my mother lit candles to keep the mosquitoes away and we sat watching the fireflies, listening to the chatter of crickets, inhaling the scent of citronella.

My sisters and I celebrate our good fortune in having each other still. We can't sing anymore, but we rejoice in our harmony, sweeter now than ever before.

—*Bluma Schwarz*

# Party Night,
# Excellent Night

You will turn thirty soon. But that is impossible. It is impossible because you are my little sister, my *baby* sister, and baby sisters aren't thirty years old.

No—it can't be. Because . . .

I am three and a half years old, and when Mommy and Daddy bring you home from the hospital, I beg them to let me hold the baby. They tell me to sit still on the couch, and then they place a bundle gently in my arms, telling me to be very, very careful. I look up into the camera, beaming, as they snap a picture. This is my baby sister, and I am old enough and responsible enough to hold her in my lap.

I am nine and you are five, and I am the first one awake in the house. It is early in the morning, and I tiptoe into your room, plotting. As you lie there asleep, I move in close and pry open your eyelid, stifling a laugh at how your eyeball stares straight up at nothing. When you wake up, I become a tormentor, pretending to be an angel that has come and taken your big sister away, or I sit on you and pin your arms back, tickling your face with my long red hair. I tease you, torture you, morning after morning, but you never tell. This is our morning routine for years.

I am ten and you are six, and we are playing tetherball in our aunt's backyard during a family picnic. We are excited, bubbling over, because we are going to stay up late, way past dark, and we are making up a song about it, a song we will sing for many years: "Party night, excellent night, / All right, / Dance the night away." We take turns doing a celebratory dance, two *Solid Gold* dancers taking a break from tetherball.

I am eleven and you are seven, and we have trekked purposefully into the field on the hill behind the house, where the grass is so tall it envelops us. We stomp it down, creating mazes, and spend an afternoon losing and finding each other over and over again. When the weather cools and the snow falls, we drag our sleds to the top of this same hill and create bobsled runs, whizzing down the trail with Olympic gold medal glory awaiting us at the bottom.

I am in seventh grade and you are in third, and we are moving to a new town. I have been sobbing for months, frightened to tears of a new school and hallways filled with strangers. You are not the shy one, you are not scared, but you side with me anyway and help me plot ways to scare people away from buying our house so we can stay there forever.

I am in eighth grade and you are in fourth, and I can make you snort milk out of your nose just by saying, "Don't laugh," as soon as you take a sip. We have a new pool in the backyard, and we are synchronized swimmers, Olympic gold medal glory materializing in new ways during the summer. We create music videos while doing our chores, turning a vacuum cleaner hose into a microphone, striking serious, sexy model poses, and taking pictures with our point-and-shoot camera. And we are very, very careful at night, wary of the ghost that lives upstairs, somewhere near our bedrooms.

I am in high school and you are in middle school, and I have my first serious boyfriend and you are convinced we will get married. You scrawl my initials and his onto your bedroom door in silver marker and lace a heart around the outside. (Years later I married a different guy, someone you like more than my high school love. Not long ago, I laughed as I showed the silly silver initials—still as bright as the day you wrote them—to my husband.)

I am leaving for college and you are entering high school. I write you letters from a boring freshman lecture. You come to my dorm for a weekend visit, and my friends and I curl your hair and sweep makeup on your face, hoping the mascara and blush will somehow mask the shiny braces and your fourteen-year-old features. A phony college ID and a dimly lit room later, we successfully sneak you into a fraternity party—and you thank us by stealing all the dances while we marvel from the sidelines.

I am graduating college and moving back home, and it is your turn to leave for dorm life. I visit you at college and carefully interview the boys you party with, ensuring they will protect and respect you. We learn to ski together on powder-covered New Hampshire slopes, sometimes inviting Dad, sometimes inviting your newest boyfriend.

I am caught up in the whirlwind of life, a blur of time and events. You quit college and move back home, and we are back together again, briefly. . . . You are pregnant and leave home, and I feel for a few months as though my baby sister has died, as if the sister I had known is gone, replaced by a different person, bitter and defensive. . . . We meet for lunch to patch a relationship. . . . We throw a surprise twenty-fifth anniversary party for Mom and Dad. . . . We celebrate your twenty-first birthday with nonalcoholic drinks, for you are pregnant. . . . You give birth to a wonderful little boy, a redheaded, freckle-faced kid who breathes new life into our family. . . . Eventually, you return home, then move out again, start a new life—rediscover yourself again and again.

I am an aunt and you are a mother. And still we pop our favorite comedy into the VCR and recite our favorite lines simultaneously, laughing until we snarf soda out of our noses. We stay up way past our bedtimes, singing "Party Night, Excellent Night" and telling stories.

I am spotting gray hairs and plucking them, and you are turning thirty. And still, you are my baby sister. And we will celebrate. Perhaps we will grab a sled and go racing down a hill, one last shot at gold medal glory. Or maybe we will take our authentic IDs—not that anyone checks them anymore—and have a real drink this time. I will interview any men we meet to make sure they will protect and respect you.

Now, I am the big sister of a thirty-year-old woman. And I realize it is okay. So we will throw you a party and laugh a lot, and we'll reminisce, if we find time for it amidst the laughter. It will be a party night, an excellent night, and we just might dance the night away.

—*Karin Crompton DiMauro*

# Tramps of the
# Neighborhood

ocation, location, location: the top three fac-
tors to consider in purchasing real estate.
Dad had a gift for predicting such properties. When
he found the lot on which to build our house in
1960, could he have clairvoyantly known we would
be positioned perfectly between the two trampolines
in our neighborhood?

By the time I was eight, both the Nicholses' and
the Coolidges' turquoise-framed, tummy-tickling
bouncing contraptions were available to any well-
behaving neighbors as long as the owners' okay was
given at the back door. My sister, Holly, and I would
scramble off the school bus and scurry up the
driveway, our plaid, vinyl book bags dangling from
shoulder straps and slapping our thighs. Uniforms
hung up, or more likely flung up, and saddle oxfords
exchanged for sneakers, we'd slow down only long

enough to grab a couple of fudge-striped cookies as we rounded the kitchen on our way out the back door. Whoever managed to peel ahead determined whether we headed right or left.

Panting upon arrival at either neighbor's threshold, we rarely had to actually ring the bell. The kitchen door was always open, allowing us to press our faces up against the screen door and, shielding our eyes to peer inside, to politely yell for the resident June Cleaver. The matron saint within always appeared thrilled to have the local urchins shatter the peace of a perfectly lovely afternoon. Kicking off our shoes as we ran into the backyard, we'd vault the frame, skim the springs, and somersault onto the warm black canvas of the tramp. Thus began an hour or two of seat wars, add-ons, and attempts to touch the clouds. We laughed at our statically charged hairdos, which only barely compensated for the intentional shocks we inflicted upon each other with skin-to-skin contact.

One afternoon, Holly and I had rotated through our bag of tricks and settled on the one-two-three seat game, which involved three simultaneous jumps followed by a seat drop. A successful attempt involved one jumper "seat-dropping" a millisecond after the other, thereby catapulting herself to the moon. That day, our timing was perfect. Featherweight Holly sprouted wings and grew smaller as she soared into the sky. Delighted with my send-off, I waited patiently for her return to earth. Suddenly, I realized I was locked on to her radar like a homing device and there was no time for clearance. My smile faded quickly as she came down on my bony knee and flounced limply like a rag doll on her side. Her eyes, big as saucers, projected fear and panic. With a barely audible whisper, she pointed to her stomach and mouthed, *I can't breathe.*

I bolted off the blasted kid killer, leapt over my shoes, and began tearing down the driveway, toward help, toward home. My sister was dying! By the time I reached the Coolidges' mailbox, I heard Holly yell, "Di, come back!" The fact that she had a voice and one that could hail me from the end of the driveway reassured me that she would live. I let the wind out of my sails as quickly as I had knocked it out of her, turned around, and awkwardly padded back in my sock feet, seeking forgiveness and pledging servant-hood for the next month for having nearly killed her.

Our "spring" fever abated after that incident and we traded the trampoline beds for flower beds. It was during our hopping hiatus that we'd discovered the Secret Garden. The backyard of Mr. and Mrs. Wilson's corner lot at the end of the street was pri-vatized by an ivy-covered brick wall. The white arched gate, with its black wrought-iron latch and hinges, beckoned the imaginations of two princesses in training. Fortunately, the Wilsons were bridge buddies of my parents, and one phone call from Mom extended our domain to yet another yard in the neighborhood.

So it was that one warm Saturday afternoon Holly and I slipped bologna-and-cheese sandwiches into fold-over sandwich bags, filled the red thermos with cherry Kool-Aid, and counted out the ever faithful fudge-striped cookies to complete our picnic lunch. Stepping off the back stoop and into character, we meandered up Marne Drive, deciding who would find the imaginary key that would open the gate to the Secret Garden. We started at the far end of the Wilsons' yard, feeling our way along the ivy-covered wall, looking for the opening, pretending not to see the gleaming white door a few feet away. Alas! The gate! Creaking on its jet-black hinges, the door swung open, revealing a scene not unlike Dorothy's view when she stepped timidly out of the fallen house onto the grounds of Munchkinland. Actually, our imaginations contributed a few colors and exotic flowers to the hydrangeas and marigolds, which were surrounded by a thick border of monkey grass. For our purposes, though, we were transported to another time and place. Who knew what magic lay within this wonderland?

We chose a patch of mossy carpet beneath a wide shade tree, sat down with our knees tucked daintily to one side, and with pinky fingers extended, began to nibble our sandwiches. Bologna has never tasted so exquisite, nor has Kool-Aid ever gone down so smoothly. Within fifteen minutes we had finished lunch, crumpled up our bags, and decided that sitting too long on ground, no matter how soft, made for itchy legs. Only once did I see the reflection of Mrs. Wilson's glasses at the kitchen window flash our way.

The fantasy was beginning to fade when my eyes caught another bright reflection in the sun, over on the patio table, right behind the citronella candle. There, like treasure begging to be discovered, lay a handful of chocolate kisses, soft from the warmth of the sun and intended for the Secret Garden girls. A gold mine, a jackpot! Again, I thought I caught a flash from the window. Only this time, it was Mrs. Wilson's smile rather than her glasses. We chose not to risk melted chocolate lining our pockets and promptly popped one after another down our gullets until all that was left was the silver foil, reduced to a small ball in my sweaty palm.

Just as we decided to exit the secret gate that had gained us entrance to the Secret Garden, the French doors to the patio flew open and there stood Mrs. Wilson, inviting us in for a quick visit before we headed back down the street. Obliging our gracious hostess, we came into her den and thanked her profusely for letting us invade her garden sanctuary, knowing how pleased Mom would be with our manners. Suspecting there was more than sugar and spice and everything nice in our healthy little frames—maybe even a few wild hairs in those pageboy haircuts of ours—she directed us down the basement stairs. She promptly introduced us to the highlight of our excursion, causing the Secret Garden to pale in comparison: a 1968, state-of-the-art, motorized Exercycle. Then Mrs. Wilson turned on her heel and headed back up the stairs, leaving us to our own devices (or rather, demises), tossing over her shoulder a nonchalant, "Have fun, but be careful!"

The bike was plugged in, and we were charged up. Being as I was still at the tail end of my servant status for having impaled Holly with my knee on the trampoline, I conceded to let her have the first turn. She crawled up, unaware the seat was adjustable and could have been lowered (had we known how) to at least come close to accommodating her preadolescent body. There was no time for fine-tuning.

Holly reached precariously out in front of her to grab the handlebars, her torso parallel with the floor. Assuming she was in place and ready to roll, I flipped the switch and realized, in an instant, that my term of service to Holly was about to be renewed. Unlike stationary bikes in the new millennium, the handlebars of the sixties were designed to move as one piece, rather than in synch with the opposite foot. No part of Holly's body was moving in conjunction with another.

The seat of the bike moved backward as the handle-bars moved forward and the pedals mechanically rotated round and round. This completely unnatural gyration yanked Holly's arms out of their sockets and whipped her neck backward, while her legs tried desperately to keep up with the wicked-witch-of-the-west pedals. Neither one of us could breathe, she from fear of being chewed up and spit out of the contraption and me from gut-busting guffaws.

Since childhood, Holly has suffered from horrendous neck aches. The doctors and chiropractors have always attributed it to a misaligned jaw. Me? I know better. It was the Wilsons' bike.

On the surface our neighborhood appeared to be a safe place to raise a family. Holly and I, however, are living proof that danger lurked around every corner. In a few weeks' time, she had the wind knocked out of her, her arms nearly dislocated, her neck whiplashed, and her disks slipped, and my stomach muscles had been strained to a crippling effect. Local residents observed us limping down the street with tear-streaked faces. Perhaps only Mrs. Wilson knew the truth: Ours were tears of laughter and the injuries self-inflicted. Go ahead—lock me up! Just make sure Holly is with me.

—Diana Parks

# Changing Currents

*1957—Little Sister*

"Maaaaaaaaa! Tell her she can't go," Kit screeched. "She's putting on her bathing suit like she's going with us. Tell her no. She's a big baby and follows me around all the time. She stinks, too."

*Oh, sure, I'm the baby,* I thought. *She's the one who can't climb a tree and who's too scared to catch bees in a jar. All she wants to do is hang around with her friends and play paper dolls. Like hanging a piece of paper on a piece of cardboard is any fun.*

"Of course, Bobbi is going," Mom said. "It's too hot to be indoors, and she is your sister. And how many times do I have to tell you? Don't call me 'Ma.' Call me 'Mom' or even 'Hey, you,' but not 'Maaaaaaaaa.' And your sister does not stink."

*Ha!* I thought as I tucked my towel under my arm

and stuck out my tongue at Kit and our cousin Dee. *Those two think they're so big because they'll be in fifth grade when school starts and have a man for a teacher. I bet third grade is as good as fifth, and he's probably mean and gives a ton of homework anyway.*

As we headed to the creek, I skipped ahead, eagerly anticipating the cool water, knowing it would take the itch out of the mosquito bites scattered across my body. But I still overheard Kit and Dee talking about how they were going to dive in the water and swim to the deep part, maybe even all the way across. How when you're in fifth grade you can swim in deep water, not like third grade babies who wash their face in gravy.

Minutes later we were all walking down the path to the bank of the creek. I found a spot for my towel and marked it with a big rock that shimmered in the sun. While Kit and Dee tried to find a place to put their stuff (as far from mine as possible), I waded into the water, the sudden cold taking my breath away. With a gasp and a shudder, I held my nose and submerged my whole body. That's the only way to do it. Get it done quickly. Next thing I knew I was holding on to "home," the big rock in the middle of the creek marking the beginning of the deep part, and laughing as I watched Kit and Dee dipping in their toes and shrieking as if the cold water were a surprise. I splashed and kicked my feet, sending wavelets of cold water toward them, grinning as they ran for the bank to lie on their towels in the sun.

## 1965—Middle Sister

Big families weren't unusual when I was a kid, so when our parents told us another baby was coming, we weren't surprised. The new one would make six, and after having been told there'd be another baby so many times, the drama kind of goes out of it. A baby was their problem, not mine.

At seventeen and fifteen, Kit and I had little inter-action with our three younger brothers. Sure, the boys were a pain and we had to babysit sometimes, but that was just normal. I assumed the new addition to our family would be another boy, and I was glad when Dad told us we had a new baby sister to even things out.

Lisa was a cute little thing, and it was fun changing and feeding her. I liked to hold her, smell the sweet scent of baby hair, and feel the comfort of her warm little body in my arms. When Mom went back to work, I became the designated babysitter. "No sense in paying someone when you have a daughter handy," our folks said. I was selected because Kit had a job and about the only time I saw her was when she came bursting into our bedroom carrying bags of new clothes, rushing to get ready for another date.

I thought nothing of it when Mom told me that Lisa had a doctor's appointment and I would be taking her. Walking along, I adjusted the carriage visor to keep the sun out of Lisa's eyes and removed the blanket to keep her cool. *She sure is pretty,* I thought, noticing her blond hair and blue eyes set off by the bonnet and matching yellow dress I had selected.

Arriving at the doctor's office, I lifted her gently out of the carriage, struggling to hold her and the diaper bag as I entered the office. The easy chatter I heard as I approached the door quieted suddenly as we entered the room. I stopped in my tracks and looked around. Everything seemed normal enough. All but two chairs lining the walls of the room were filled with women holding their babies, waiting to see the doctor.

"We have a one-thirty appointment," I told the receptionist.

"Take a seat and I'll call you when the doctor can see you," she said.

Several women snapped back into place as I turned to take my seat. They had been whispering to one another, looking first at Lisa and then at me.

*What's going on?* I wondered. *What's wrong with these people?*

As the minutes ticked by, the women remained silent and thin-lipped. I could feel the pressure building in the room as they rocked and shushed and fed their infants. Every so often one of them would whisper to another and shake her head sadly. Finally, the woman to my left, the one who had done the most whispering and head shaking, leaned over to me.

"Your baby looks just like you," she said.

"Oh, thank you," I replied, "but she isn't my baby. She's my sister."

The woman's eyes opened wide in surprise and her mouth relaxed into a smile. Realization finally hit me. My face flamed red as the tension eased out of the room with an audible sigh. When the receptionist called us to see the doctor, I retreated to the examining room, loving Lisa and wanting her to disappear all at the same time.

## 1987—Big Sister

"Are you alone?" Mom asked, her voice cracking over the phone.

"Why, what's wrong?"

"Can you get someone to come over and stay with you?"

"No. What is it?"

"It's bad," she said.

"Mom, please, you're scaring me."

"It's Kitty. She's gone. She died last night."

I couldn't breathe. My heart thumped wildly in double time. Pinpoints of light danced in front of my eyes as the floor came up and hit me in the ass. My mind whirled in anguished confusion: *This can't be. It's a mistake, a nightmare, a stupid prank by some* demented person pretending to be my mother. It's not real. Not Kitty. Not my big sister—vibrant, irreverent, flipping her middle finger to the world as she embraced life, flaunting her long silky legs in outfits I never would dare to wear.

But it was true. In an instant of unimaginable tragedy, Kitty was gone, forever.

*How dare you, God?* I raged. *How dare you create this hole in our lives, rearranging the order of things? Don't you see? I can't be the big sister. I still need my big sister.*

Until I lost my big sister, I didn't realize that by jumping in ahead, I had actually been following her lead.

## 2002—Sisters

As the years passed, it was easy to lose touch with my family. I had my hands full raising my four kids as a single parent on a shoestring budget. Long-distance calls cost a lot, visits cost a lot more, and I could never find the time to write. Who wanted to hear my woes, anyway? Even when things got better, a lot better after I got married again, there didn't seem to be a way to reconnect. Too much time had passed. Lisa had grown up, had a family of her own. She had moved on without me. Then Mom got sick.

I felt the pressure building in my ears as the plane began its descent. Minutes after arriving, I spotted Lisa waiting for me at baggage claim, still blond, blue-eyed, and beautiful. I had a hard time imagining that this was once the baby girl I carried into the doctor's office in front of all those disapproving women.

Throughout our mother's illness, Lisa had been taking care of both her own family and Mom. I'd taken a leave of absence from my job to give her a bit of a break and a shoulder to lean on.

With a quick embrace and a warm smile, Lisa welcomed me as I grabbed my bag, and we headed off immediately for a meeting with Mom's doctor. The diagnosis of non-Hodgkin's lymphoma was frightening and way overdue in coming, but now the ugly thing debilitating our mother finally had a name.

"What we are dealing with is a very large and aggressive tumor that has wrapped around your internal organs," the doctor stated bluntly.

I swallowed hard and looked at Mom to see her reaction. Only her whitened knuckles grasping her chair showed any indication of fear. *She is so strong,* I thought, praying that fortitude would carry her through.

The chemotherapy was brutal, but Mom hung in there. One of her five kids was always with her, with Lisa and me taking the longer shifts, prompting the visiting priest to dub us her "guardian angels." We questioned treatments, tracked doctor visits, watered flowers, cleaned Mom's teeth, even wiped her bottom. And we talked, with our mother and with each other.

Sometimes long into the night, getting to know one another again. Finding out how very much alike we really are. Connecting in the knowledge that we would do everything to help Mom.

For a time things looked very bad. For four horrific days Mom was completely unresponsive. She didn't seem to know we were there, didn't notice the vigil held by her children or that her vast extended family moved in and out of the room, praying for her, willing her to come through. With heavy hearts we began to realize we might lose her. Exhausted, Lisa and I agreed to go to dinner with our cousin Dee.

As we left the room, I leaned over and whispered, "We're going to get something to eat, Mom. We'll be right back."

Thinking I'd seen her eyelids flicker slightly in response, I waited, looking intently at her eyes as I held my breath. But she remained motionless, eyes closed, and I realized it was just an illusion, a product of my own need for hope.

Sadly, we left her side. The three of us tried to maintain a positive attitude during dinner, but as we made our way back to the hospital, each of us was silently bracing for the worst and trying to hold up for the others. When we returned, we found Mom lying peacefully in bed, exactly as she'd been when we left.

"We're back," I called as we entered the room.

"That's good," she replied.

Stunned, Lisa and I stared at the bed and then turned to Dee, who wore the same surprised look on her face. Mom slowly opened her eyes and beckoned to Lisa, who was standing closest to her.

Cupping Lisa's face in her hands, Mom kissed her and whispered, "God gave me back."

And so He had. When, over the next few days Mom improved and it began to look like we'd be able to take her home, Lisa and I knew we'd been twice blessed. We had our Mom back, and we'd found one another.

—*Bobbi Carducci*

# A Plane Ticket, a Phone Call, and a Country Song

It all started with a plane ticket and a phone call. "How'd you like a visitor the second week in July?" I asked my big sister, Deanne. I knew the answer. In fact, I had already booked my flight to Nashville.

"What? You're kidding! Dawn, that'd be great!" she exclaimed in her impossible-to-place accent.

We've been told we sound alike. I find that extremely odd, since I speak like the stereotypical Long Island girl, while her accent is a smattering of all the places she's lived—Southern California, New York, Tennessee, and a bit of God-knows-what-else thrown in.

I shared the details of my trip with Deanne. The owner of the publishing company where I worked as an assistant editor had just sold one of his magazines and was giving the entire company a week off and each of us a nice bonus to celebrate.

A few weeks later, Deanne picked me up at the Nashville airport. We headed straight for her rural home just outside of Paris, Tennessee. Over the next few days, I enjoyed my first genuine Southern "bar-bee-que," hung out at the local Dairy Queen with my teenage niece and nephew, and got to know the waitress at the neighborhood greasy spoon. Mostly, Deanne and I did what most sisters do when they get together—shopped and gossiped.

Then we headed back to Nashville, just the two of us, for the rest of the vacation. By the last day of our trip, we'd seen the Country Music Hall of Fame, Ernest Tubb Record Shop, and Studio B on Music Row. I'm not sure how two girls born and raised in the suburbs of New York grew up with an affinity for country music. Perhaps it had something to do with our dad singing George Jones and Kenny Rogers every morning while he shaved.

After a long day of touring country music land-marks, we sat in Nashville's Red Roof Inn downing TGI Friday's mudslides from little plastic cups. We poured them straight from the bottle, no blender, no ice, just sweet chocolatey rum. I gazed out the window at the burning Nashville sun, grateful both for the air conditioning and that our trip had been blessed with such good weather. Even with the constant humidity hanging in the air, we hadn't seen one drop of rain.

"We should go to the Grand Ole Opry," I suddenly blurted out.

Deanne smirked at me. Between our dinner at Ruth's Chris Steakhouse and five days of nonstop shopping, the trip had already broken both our banks and then some.

"Seriously," I said, jumping up from the bed and grabbing the stack of tourist brochures we'd picked up in the hotel lobby. "I want to go to the Opry."

"That'd be cool," Deanne said in a voice that warned me not to get my hopes up.

Tickets would probably be expensive, sold out, or both. But my quest had already begun. She shrugged as I dialed the phone.

"Do you have any tickets available for tonight?" I asked. I caught Deanne's eye and a wide grin spread across my face. "Thank you. We'll be there." I gave the girl my name and thanked her again.

"Well?"

"They have tickets, only twenty dollars. Our reservations are set. We pay at the door."

Deanne silently performed calculations in her head. "Let's do it," she said finally.

My hands trembled with excitement, and I couldn't keep still. I paced the room to burn off the nervous energy. "We're going to the Opry! We're going to the Opry!" I chanted, the thought dancing in my mind like the refrain of a song.

"Who's playing?" Deanne asked, catching my enthusiasm.

I opened the trifold brochure and hunted for the correct date. I skimmed through a few lesser-known names that sounded vaguely familiar, then got to the current stars. "Terri Clark. Steve Wariner—"

"Steve Wariner!" we squealed in unison.

"He'd better play 'Two Teardrops,'" I said.

"I hope he does 'Kansas City Lights.' Do you think he will?" Deanne asked. At my blank stare, she added, "Oh, that one was from before you were born."

"I've heard of it," I said indignantly, the little sister never wanting to be shown up or left out. A favorite tune sprung to my mind. "If he plays 'Holes in the Floor of Heaven,' I'm going to cry," I said.

"Yeah," Deanne said, matching my somber tone. "I love that song."

The song, a Top Forty hit on country radio stations at the time, traces the stages of a man's life as he loses first his grandmother, then his wife. The falling rain in the chorus symbolizes the tears cried by loved ones who have passed on.

I thought of our own family's beliefs. We've always told the younger children that Nana and Grandpa watch us from stars in the sky. Many nights, I would look up in the sky, find the two brightest stars, and know Mommy and Daddy were looking after me.

"Well, let's get ready," I said, opening my suitcase to get my sister's opinion on a choice of outfits.

Hours later, we stepped into the Opry and found our seats amidst the rows of red velvet chairs. I'd been in theaters both larger and more impressive but few exuding as much history and tradition.

"Daddy would have loved this city," I said. "This theater, the Hall of Fame, everything. I can't believe he never made it here."

There were too many cities that our dad, who died of a heart attack at fifty-two, had never seen. By the time I was twenty-three, I'd already been to Chicago, Nashville, San Diego, Orlando, San Antonio, and New York. Over the next five years, I added Anaheim; Albany; Cleveland; Washington, D.C.; Baltimore; Key West; and Sydney, Australia, to the list.

"Fifty-two was so young," I said to Deanne, a sudden realization.

Looking at my sister's face, I had another realization: She's nearly forty. And I'm reminded that she's got our mother's eyes. In the picture of Deanne hanging on my living room wall, she is dressed in her U.S. Navy blues, young and smiling, holding a squirming two-year-old—me. That photo represents one of the few recollections I have of her as a child. I barely knew her growing up. She left for the Navy when I was three, came back as a stranger when I was six. For many years, she was a voice on the telephone with which I felt a vague, tenuous connection. But as time goes by, a sixteen-year age difference shrinks to a blip. Strangers grow into sisters, then into friends and finally confidantes. In Nashville, sitting together drinking diet Pepsi from collectible mugs and listening to music that crosses generations, we became contemporaries.

I felt my heart pounding in my chest as I looked down and saw him—the star, Steve Wariner—a tiny figure from that distance. Deanne and I sang along to each of his songs, dancing and clapping during the bluesy "Burning the Roadhouse Down."

Then we heard the telling first chords and the emotional first line: *One day shy of eight years old, my grandma passed away. . . .*

My sister looked over at me. A lump grew in my throat. By the end of the first verse, the tears in my eyes had burst into two streams pouring down my face. Deanne grabbed my hand. Thankful for the contact, I gripped hers tighter. We sat there, two sisters, fully grown orphans, alone and together. Identical tears fell from identical blue eyes down identical round, rosy cheeks. We sat, wordlessly, motionless, holding hands, listening and feeling every note, every word.

When the song ended, we sniffled simultaneously, wiped our tears, and enjoyed the rest of the show, saying nothing more about the song. Bittersweet smiles said all that needed to be said. And yes, he did sing "Kansas City Lights." And yes, I knew the song.

After the concert, we sat on a bench in front of the Opry, resting our feet and enjoying the waning sun as the traffic dissipated. I shivered as I felt the slightest tickle of something wet on my bare arms.

"Did you feel that?" Deanne asked.

I had felt it, too, but had dismissed it as my imagination. I looked down at the pavement, speckled with freshly fallen drops. Aside from a few fluffy clouds over the Opry, the sky remained sunny and blue.

"Yes, I did," I said, smiling. "Mommy and Daddy must be watching."

—Dawn Allcot

# Silly Little Prayer

"Are you awake?"

Even though the room was dark, Moni could sense I wasn't asleep yet by the rate at which I tossed and turned trying to get comfortable.

"Are you awake?" she repeated with the urgency of a good joke waiting to be told.

Growing up with my younger sister as a room-mate often made me wish I had my own room. When I entered my teens, the bunk beds we'd slept on as little girls were replaced by a daybed with a trundle. Moni got the daybed. I got the trundle, which actually was a mattress on wheels that set a few inches above the floor. With Moni's Barbies and play clothes strewn along the carpet, it was hard to relax on this makeshift bed that occupied three-fourths of the room's walking space. Plus, the daybed towered over my trundle, so Moni could easily peek down at me as we lay in our beds at night.

I turned my head to look up at her shadowed face. "Yeah, I'm awake." I answered her. "So?"

"Well, I can't sleep. Do you want to talk?"

"About what?" I groaned.

Moni's small talk was not my idea of fun at ten o'clock on a school night.

"Let's say 'Goodnight, Goodnight,'" she said.

Moni and I started saying "Goodnight, Goodnight" as a way to lull ourselves to sleep when we were little girls and had continued doing so almost every night. Moni repeated after me as I said this little prayer, which sounded like a two-part harmony:

> *Goodnight . . .*
> *Goodnight . . .*
> *I love you . . .*
> *I love you . . .*
> *Too . . .*
> *Too . . .*
> *Forever . . .*
> *Forever*
> *No matter what we do. . . .*
> *No matter what we do. . . .*
> *I love . . .*

At that point in the prayer, we spouted off the names of all the famous guys we loved at the time.

"I love," we each repeated, "Tom Cruise, Kirk Cameron, and Corey Haim."

"Don't forget Corey Feldman," Moni said. She liked the rebellious teen stars.

Satisfied, she turned to face the wall, and within a couple of minutes, I could hear her faint snore.

I lay there wide awake for a long time, our prayer humming through my mind. What annoyed me most about sharing a room was that I usually was the last one to fall asleep. That night, Moni slept soundly while I kept hearing "Corey Feldman" in my head.

Sharing a room caused a lot of envy on my part. Not only did Moni get the best bed in the room, but she also had the enviable position of being the youngest child in the family. With her sky blue eyes and golden blond hair, she was the stereotypical beautiful youngest sibling who could wrap my parents around her finger and drive me crazy at the same time.

At age ten, she swiped a pack of cigarettes from my parents' bedroom without them knowing and invited a neighborhood girl to our room for a few drags. An empty Marlboro Lights package buried in the bedroom trash can was my clue.

She made a fashion statement at school when she borrowed my clothes without asking and mixed and matched them with creative flair. She left her indelible mark on them: holes where the shoulder pads had been cut out of my shirts.

Moni knew how to have fun and, as the person who slept just a few feet away, I had no choice but to watch her. Her resting body was in sharp contrast to mine. She was totally peaceful, each breath she exhaled seeming to relax her even more.

Meanwhile, still awake, I tensed my fists and leg muscles and slowly released them, an exercise I had once been told relieves insomnia. My sleep was often hindered by my worries: Was I doing a good enough job in school? Did my parents approve of my behavior? Was I practicing everything I had been taught in church that Sunday? While Moni enjoyed her mischievous escapades, I put my efforts into finishing homework first thing on Friday nights so I could relax the rest of the weekend. But, unlike Moni, I had trouble relaxing, because I was usually worried about something. I continued tensing and relaxing my body until it made me somewhat drowsy.

"Are you still awake?" Moni's words, though spoken quietly, pierced through the nighttime silence.

My stomach had already begun to ache from the sheer stress of not being able to fall asleep. The fear of being the only person awake in the house had made me even more anxious. Being an insomniac is lonely.

"Nope," I sighed. "Not yet."

It's true that I longed to have my own room—a spacious bed, my own closet, dresser drawers filled with clothes without holes in the shoulders. I resented sharing a room with my sister and longed for the personal space that being a teenager entitled me to. Still, that night, I didn't mind hearing Moni's voice.

Perhaps I had come to depend on sharing a room and having a sister to talk to at any hour of the night. Moni, after all, provided my life with much-needed adventure.

"Would you like to say it again?" I asked.

By "it" I was referring to the words that oddly connected me to my sister despite my envy and little annoyances with her.

> *Goodnight . . .*
> *I love you . . .*
> *Too . . .*
> *Forever . . .*
> *No matter what we do . . .*

Many years have passed since Moni and I shared that room. Sometimes when I'm lying awake at night, the words that used to be spoken by two sisters are now spoken alone. I repeat "Goodnight, Goodnight" to myself as if I'm still thirteen years old. Only this time, the list of "famous" people I love is a little more realistic: my husband, our two-year-old son, my parents, and a childhood pal named Tom Cruise.

Though she lives many miles from me, I believe Moni, too, is lying awake and saying those words right back to me. Our silly little prayer. Funny how it can bridge the miles and the very different personalities between two sisters.

—Shanna Bartlett Groves

# Come What May

Some early Christmas present the long-distance phone call had been. My mother, still lecturing, writing, and traveling well into her eighties, had suffered a massive stroke.

I crossed the sterile whiteness of the hospital room, unbroken except for a bird of paradise arrangement and two poinsettias on the window ledge, and leaned over my mother's bed to kiss her cheek.

"Hi, Mom," I said. "How are you?"

Mother was as pale as the hospital linens tucked around her. Her eyes registered recognition, but the paralysis prevented any speech. I wondered how much of her keen intellect was as frozen as her body. Then the bedding rustled and lifted where, I realized, her big toe must be. Apparently she had this one movement left to her, and with it she signaled a greeting.

My sister Jackie sat by the bed, her cheeks

smudged black where rivers of tears had spread her mascara.

"How was your flight?" she asked, her voice subdued.

"I couldn't get an earlier plane," I said. Not an answer to her question. Reeling from the sight of my mother, I was already defensive with my sister. Apparently tragedies didn't alter basic family dynamics.

I hadn't felt close to Jackie for years. Decades, really. We kept in touch through Christmas cards, token gifts, and maybe an annual or biannual phone call. That was it. Funny, it would be time for the perfunctory card and gift in another month, but here we were, face-to-face. We'd have to actually talk.

"I got here in less than an hour when Dad called. He's home now, getting some sleep," Jackie said.

Jackie lived close by and did a thousand things more for Mother than I. She'd been at the hospital for a good twenty hours already. I was the daughter come lately. I was grateful to Jackie, of course. But I felt a mixture of jealousy and shame too. If there'd been a contest for best daughter, she would have won.

Once upon a time Jackie and I had been devoted sisters. She was adopted, and I wasn't, but who cared? I worshiped her with the adulation of a younger sister who wants to tag along for everything. I whined for her to play with me and begged her for help with a thousand things. We entertained relatives and neighbors as a dance duo when I was three and she was six. All through elementary school we tossed socks between our twin beds at night and whispered secrets of the boy we had a crush on. We tugged the wishbone at Thanksgiving, hunted candy treasures at Easter, and shared the backseat of the family car on hot stretches across the Nevada and Utah desert to visit relatives every summer. She helped me get ready for my first date, carefully stuffing toilet paper into my bra, applying a dab of lipstick to my lips, and sending me off with the considerable advice of someone three years older and much wiser.

Growing up, we'd supported each other through times of worry and grief too. Judy came to mind. Not that I was comparing Mother to a German shepherd; Jackie and I had never faced anything like Mother's stroke. But we had loved our dog, Judy, as much as any friend. A large painting of her still hung in the dining room of my parents' home. When Judy got hurt, my sister and I knelt by our maple twin beds and prayed for her recovery. She died despite our prayers, and we sobbed in each other's arms.

When had we stopped being devoted sisters and started our constant bickering?

By the time we were teens, my mother was already slumping to the kitchen table several times a week, putting her head in her hands and complaining that we were giving her a migraine. Had it begun when we went to Utah without my parents and my sister spent a lot of time with her birth father? I would have been ten, she thirteen. She came home from that trip telling everyone I was her cousin, not her sister. Sure, she was adopted, but she'd always been loved as much as me. Actually, in my opinion, more. I hated her telling that story.

Or did our rivalry simply arise from the myriad competitions of siblings—for the prettiest doll, the nicest dress, the easiest chores? In other families, these petty grievances resolved themselves with maturity. Ours seemed to have grown into some kind of feud, like the malignant cells of a deadly tumor.

I pulled up a chair opposite Jackie and reached for Mother's hand, messaging it gently, willing life into the cold, limp fingers.

"It's already December," I said. "You'll have to get well fast, Mom. I'll fly down with the kids and we can celebrate both Christmas Eve and Christmas Day."

Mother raised the bedding in agreement. I thought her eyes smiled.

"I'll make dinner on Christmas," Jackie offered.

"I make a mean turkey. I could do that part," I said. "Or I could fix a ham."

"I make turkey too. You don't have to bother."

"You make the menu. I'll pitch in however you want when I get here," I said. "You're the real home-maker anyway."

I meant it as a sincere compliment. She winced as though I was pelting her with sarcasm.

"You are a consummate homemaker," I elaborated, backtracking. "I wish my house ever looked as nice as yours."

"I didn't think you noticed or cared," she said softly. "A nice house is important to me. It isn't important to you."

I wanted to hit her, but I wasn't a child anymore. At least I hoped I wasn't. Of course I had noticed. Of course I cared. Like Jackie, I, too, had been raised to value a beautiful home. My kids would love a cookie jar filled with homemade cookies like hers enjoyed; my husband would love carpets vacuumed more than once a month. But between teaching full time and chauffeuring three kids to a host of activities, some days I couldn't find ten minutes to tackle the mound of laundry waiting on the couch to be folded or the dishes growing green stuff in the sink. Jackie had no idea how often I felt awash with inadequacies. When Jackie did take a break from the hospital, she would probably spend her time creating a gingerbread house for the approaching festivities. I would do well to purchase and hang a supermarket wreath when I went home.

I pried open my heart and looked again at Jackie. Everything about her, from red eyes to rumpled clothes, radiated misery. She wasn't arguing at all.

She was stating what she considered a fact.

"You are so accomplished," Jackie said. "You always have been. You write. You teach school. You do all the things Mother and Daddy did."

"You have twice as many kids as me and still do it all," I countered. "And you do the things the church teaches us we should do."

"Maybe if I was your real sister I'd be more like you."

Astonishment silenced me for a moment. "You are my real sister," I finally said. "I had no idea how you felt."

I tucked Mother's hand under the covers, walked over to Jackie's chair, and drew her into a long hug. My shoulder grew wet where she pressed her face against it. How had I missed, for so long, her feelings of inadequacy? Gingerbread houses were the last thing on her mind. We actually had something very deep and fundamental in common: the sense of not being good enough, the fear of not being loved.

"I have something," Jackie said. From a sack by her chair she pulled out a pudgy, fawn-colored stuffed German shepherd.

"Mother will love that," I said. "It looks like Judy."

"This isn't for Mother. I bought it for you." She pressed the dog into my arms.

"Early Christmas," I said. "Thanks."

"It isn't for Christmas. It's just because."

Because I needed comfort. Because I could be losing my mother. Because I was here sharing this awful moment with Jackie. Because we are sisters. My eyes misted and I hugged her again. We had different interests. And the jealousy and hurt of years gone by would still bite at us sometimes. But Jackie and I did love and care about each other. Together we would get through Mother's stroke and any other tragedy that struck our family.

The bedding moved, Mother's big toe signaling her appreciation and approval. This time I know her eyes smiled.

—*Samantha Ducloux*

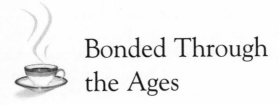

# Bonded Through the Ages

Alice was 102 years old and still living in her own home. She could not have continued to live independently unless her "baby sister," Anna, aged ninety-two, assisted her. Never married, the two sisters still lived together in the same house in which they'd been born so many years before.

I was a visiting nurse for Alice. Every time I stepped into the house, it felt like I had entered a time machine. There was an antique wood-burning Franklin stove in the center of the small living room, which served as a heat source for the home as well as for drying their freshly hand-laundered clothes. Lace doilies, yellowed with age, graced every flat surface. Crocheted afghans and antique lamps were everywhere. In fact, nothing in that house was younger than eighty years old.

The two sisters had lived in the same community

for the entire twentieth century. They had both worked in the nearby textile mill, now abandoned, a remnant of more prosperous days. Over the years, they had cared for brothers, sisters, parents, nieces, and nephews until they were the only two left in their large extended family.

When I met them, their combined weight was less than their combined age. They both wore their hair, for decades completely white, in sparse little buns on top of their heads. Their posture was stooped, and Anna helped Alice get out of her rocking chair and walk ten feet to the bathroom, a journey that took about five minutes to accomplish.

Each visit I made to their home was fascinating. My main purpose was to change the bandages on Alice's leg, where she had a chronic ulcer that first appeared twenty years earlier and recently had become infected. Anna insisted on helping me, feeling it was her duty as her sister's caregiver.

Because Alice was almost totally deaf, Anna whispered things to me in front of Alice. I had to stifle my laughter as Anna told me stories about Alice's "naughty" past or described what a "stubborn old woman" her sister had become. I couldn't help but smile at the image of Alice in a flapper dress with her ankles "exposed" in a risqué manner. I wondered how many men's hearts these women had broken in the past.

The two sisters shared a bond so close that words were unnecessary. Anna understood Alice completely and anticipated her every need. She did grumble that Alice wanted everything her way, and like most sisters, they bickered occasionally in front of me.

They slept together in the same bed, mostly to keep each other warm. Bedtime was exactly 7:00 P.M. for Alice, and though Anna complained it was much too early for her to retire each night, she went to bed at the same time so Alice would feel safe and comfortable.

I was concerned about their nutrition and ability to manage meal preparation. Anna assured me she did all of the cooking.

"Meals on Wheels is for sick old people," she said.

She proudly showed me the pantry full of oatmeal, creamed soups, and soft foods, all of which Alice was so fond. A nephew did the weekly grocery shopping for her, undoubtedly to Anna's specifications. I tried in vain to explain about the high salt content in canned soups, but my words fell on deaf ears. Who could argue with a ninety-two-year-old caring for her 102-year-old sister? I figured that if they'd lived that long on their diet, it couldn't be that harmful.

My association with the two sisters lasted only about six weeks. When Alice's leg ulcer finally healed, Anna was able to take care of her sister without outside help. I felt privileged to have been a part of their lives for those short weeks. I lost track of the sisters but heard from neighbors that they resumed their routine lifestyle without the daily visits of the town nurses. I imagine the two sisters have passed away by now, but I refuse to verify that fact. I prefer to remember them in their long, lace-collared dresses, walking together on that long ten-foot journey to the bedroom, supporting each other as they had for so many decades.

—*Alice C. Facente*

# A Fossil for Molly

I tie on a new fly to replace the one I lost to a bobbing log and cast again into the fast-moving river. My cast goes awry and the fly plunks into the water not ten feet from where I stand.

Molly would flop over in her grave. No, she'd chuckle and insist I'd had my chance to learn and flubbed it. And she'd be right.

For me, fishing hadn't been what made excursions with my big sister, Molly, so special. I went along just to be with her in the great outdoors that she called her "cathedral." She fished this river, the Owens, often, flicking effortless casts under the willows, depositing the fly slightly upstream from the particular riffle where she knew a large rainbow trout lingered. Then she waited, motionless, for a strike.

But once the trout was in her creel, Molly pointed out grasshoppers sailing noisily from one clump of long, pale-gold grass to another, orange dragonflies flitting among slender reeds at the water's edge, and deer tracks imprinted in the deep mud of the bank—the things one has to slow down to see.

Today is the fifth anniversary of her death. I've come back to the Owens, to Molly's cathedral, to do things we once did together, two sisters separated by sixteen years. This pilgrimage is a way to honor her memory, her long, brave struggle with cancer, and to recollect our times together. I've come here in hope of feeling closer to her here in the terrain she loved, where she was my confidante, my teacher, my sounding board, my advisor. Here on this river, Molly helped me understand our parents, the mother and father who both had been middle aged by the time I was born. Here, Molly eased my transition to a third grade classroom in a new school, helped me resolve a quarrel with my best friend in junior high, and consoled me when my high school boyfriend and I parted ways.

I reel in and whip another cast over my shoulder. The line catches in the top of a lacy willow behind me. I jiggle the tip of the pole to one side and then the other, harder each time, until the leader snaps, leaving my bedraggled fly hooked into an arching branch. Overhead an eagle etches a lazy spiral in the cloud-dappled sky. It cries—wild, free, fierce.

I close my eyes and remember what my wise sister taught me.

*Slow down. Concentrate. Merge with the surge of the line, the flow of the river, the cycle of the trout.*

When I open my eyes, I am staring down at the gray river-run stones at my feet. There beside the toe of my red sneaker, a rougher speckled rock commands my attention. What looks like a fossil protrudes from its top. It must have been washed out of the bank by the heavy rains this winter. Too bad Molly isn't here to share this moment.

The thought jerks me back seven years to another afternoon on this very river.

"Look at this," Molly called to me, pointing to just such a rock that lay some eight feet from where she was fishing.

"A fossil!" I cried out, gaping at gleaming white streaked with rust and dark shadows. It appeared to be the pearly interior of an oyster shell.

"It could be millions of years old," Molly said, an odd half smile flirting with her lips. "I feel a kinship to fossils. It has something to do with their age, the fact that they've been around so long." A glint shone in her eyes behind her glasses.

I had just learned about fossils in high school and was eager to grasp our find in my hands.

Molly touched my shoulder to hold me back. "Let's just admire it for a few moments," she murmured, that same smile hovering. "Think of what that fossil represents, its staying power, surviving through time by transformation.

"When I see a fossil," she continued, "I imagine the dead reborn, clothed in a new beauty, in a stability to last the ages."

At the time, we weren't aware of the cancer lurking in her lungs. That knowledge would come six months later. But for me, her long struggle and eventual death were forever linked with her description of the transformation of oyster to fossil. I like to think that my wonderful sister also had been clothed in a new beauty and would survive the ages.

On the day we found the fossil, I remained beside Molly, imagining the eons the oyster shell had lain in clay compacting to stone while shell transformed into fossil. I pictured the river wrenching it from the earth and abandoning it here for Molly and me to discover. For several minutes I admired the fossil— caught in its spell, entangled in my own good fortune, savoring the moment when I would squat beside it and run my fingers across it.

Finally, Molly and I went to claim our fossil. I took a deep breath and squatted to brush my fingertips lightly over it. They came away damp, soiled with white goo. Then I noticed my fingers had smeared white into rust and dark shadows. Startled, I inspected our find. It was merely the transient monument to the passage of a large bird. Molly hunched over, slapped her thighs, and nearly strangled with laughter.

"You knew all along," I yelped, recalling the smile and the glint. Grinning, I rinsed my fingers in the river and wiped them on my faded jeans. "I'll get even," I warned, glaring at her and then skyward, in the bird's direction.

Now, seven years later, I stand over the fossil I've just discovered. Aloft, the eagle still soars lazily, its dark wings stark against the clouds. It shrieks and shrieks again, its cry stabbing my heart like a message from Molly. Slowly, I bend over and drag my fingers across the fossil. It is not damp; the colors do not smear. The oyster shell is smooth to my touch as I trace its outline embedded in the rough stone. I glance up at the eagle and feel closer to my sister than I have in months.

Here's your fossil, Molly.

—*Ann Newton Holmes*

# Surviving Skylah

I spent most of my early childhood in my room. It wasn't that I was being confined to my room. I merely needed to protect my stuff.

Skylah was the problem. She was the bane of my existence. With her curly yellow hair and pudgy, rose-colored cheeks, she could have been the model for one of Michelangelo's cherubs. Everybody but I thought she was utterly delightful. I tried to warn our parents about the evil lurking behind those innocent, China blue eyes, but nobody would listen.

I repeatedly told our parents how Skylah would sneak into my room and steal my best toys. How she would leave a terrible mess all over the place and sometimes break things. I begged them to put a lock on my bedroom door, but they wouldn't hear of it. Instead, I was told to "make allowances" because she was younger. I wasn't sure what allowances were, but

I knew I didn't want to make them. I was left with little choice but to spend most of my time in my room, standing guard over my things.

Of course, I had to come out sometimes. Mealtimes were the main problem. I didn't eat a lot in those days, because I had to get back to my bedroom before Skylah finished her food. Fortunately, Skylah possessed a healthy appetite, so it usually wasn't a problem. Not until the day my favorite chocolate cake appeared on the table, a cake so tantalizing I couldn't resist a second slice.

She couldn't have gotten there more than two or three minutes before I did. But it was time enough. My beautiful new porcelain doll lay broken on the floor—head smashed into a thousand pieces, her silk kimono scrunched and smeared with sticky chocolate from Skylah's grubby little hands. One sad glassy gray eye stared out at me accusingly from beneath the dresser, where it had rolled.

Well, what would you have done? I smacked her smug little face, of course. And then I smacked her again, quite hard. At her screech of protest, Mother came hurrying into the room. She surveyed the wreckage with a grim expression. I thought I was in big trouble for sure, because I wasn't supposed to hit my sister—ever. But justice prevailed, that time, at least. Mother told Skylah that she deserved the slap.

I decided to push home my advantage.

"She needs to buy me a new doll."

"Yes, she certainly does," agreed Mother.

Skylah was forced to empty her piggy bank of every last coin. She'd been saving for a new gerbil and a cage to keep it in. She'd had almost enough, and now there she was, counting out her last pennies to give to her spiteful sister. Skylah sobbed broken-heartedly about it being "only an accident." I relished every clink of change as it hit the floor.

I had little time to enjoy my victory. That very evening saw Skylah in the hospital with a raging fever and a sore throat. I was left with Mrs. Nichols next door while my parents took Skylah to the hospital. When they didn't return home that night, I was afraid something really bad had happened to my sister.

The next day, my dad returned home and explained that Skylah's tonsils had been removed that morning and she was going to be fine. I didn't believe him. I thought she was dying and it was my fault because I'd made her cry. I didn't tell anybody how I felt; I couldn't get the words to come out. I spent the whole day with a really sick feeling in my tummy, sitting quietly in Mrs. Nichols's musty blue velveteen chair, pretending to read.

Skylah came home two days later. I forgot my concern for her as soon as I found out she'd gotten to eat nothing but ice cream for two whole days. Things returned to normal, and soon I was wishing there was a second pair of tonsils they could take out of my sister.

Now, why am I thinking of all this some fifty years later? Well, Skylah was recently in the hospital again, this time to remove her gallbladder. I sat by her bed while she was still a little groggy from the anesthetic.

"Jane, do you remember when I broke your china doll and you made me pay to get you a new one?" she asked.

"You never did pay," I said. "I gave you the money back. I also bought you a gerbil out of my own pocket money. It was waiting for you when you got home from having your tonsils out."

"Yeah, well . . . I broke that doll on purpose. I wanted to pay you back for being such a mean sister and not letting me play with your toys. I was a rotten little thing, wasn't I?" Her giggle was a bit groggy.

She probably didn't notice my gritted teeth as I said sweetly, "Do you have any more organs that could be removed while you're here?"

Sometimes I wonder why the two of us are such good friends.

—Margaret B. Davidson

A version of this story was published as "Sisters" in *Hodgepodge Sunny Edition*, fall 2001.

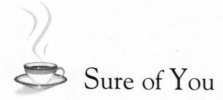 Sure of You

A coyote bayed long and sad to the late-night moon. Soon, from a place not too distant from where the three children were listening, came a mournful reply. Anna, the youngest child, began to cry.

"Be quiet, Anna, and hurry up," her brother whispered as he dashed for the ladder and scrambled up to their room in the attic. "This lantern is heavy."

Three-year-old Anna knew the hungry coyotes must be lurking in the shadowy, dark sagebrush, and she was terrified. She stepped backward, pressing herself against the wall of the house. Then she felt Ella's arms wrap around her, pulling her protectively close.

"Don't be afraid. I'm right here; I'll take care of you," she whispered.

Comforted by Ella's presence, Anna bravely dashed for the narrow wooden ladder and climbed toward the loft with Ella close behind. Once inside, Ella quickly bolted the door against the dark night. Shivering, the children hurriedly slipped into night-clothes, then hopped into the center of the fluffy feather mattress on their bed and pulled another down quilt up over their heads. Soon their shared body warmth had them feeling safe and cozy.

"See, now, the coyotes didn't get you, did they?" Ella laughed, tickling her little sister until she squirmed and giggled. "I saved you again."

Even their brother, Rudy, laughed.

Ella, being the oldest, always entertained her younger siblings with bedtime tales so sleep would come more quickly. That particular night she wanted to tell them her own special story.

"I was only eight years old when you were born, Anna," she began. "You were such a little thing, all pink and wiggly. You were wrapped so tightly in soft flannel blankets that you looked like a little butterfly in a cocoon. Everyone says newborn babies can't see, but when I touched your hand, you looked right at me and I knew you could see me with your dark eyes. Then you grabbed hold of my finger. You knew me right from the start.

"Did you know I prayed for a baby sister?" she continued. "Even before we left Germany, I wanted a sister."

Rudy snorted, pretending to be offended. He had

wanted a brother, he told them, just before Ella kicked his foot beneath the covers. He giggled, pleased to get such a rise out of his sister.

"Boys are alright for some things, Rudy," she explained, "but girls need other girls to play with. Girls don't like playing with dogs and frogs. Girls like cooking and dress-up and acting like princesses."

Rudy groaned and rolled his back to them, pretending not to listen. Anna begged to hear more.

"You were named after our grandma in Germany," Ella continued, "so your name is very special. So is mine. I was named after Mama's sister. I don't know who Rudy was named after."

Ella went on to tell Anna how she, a girl of six, had come to America with Rudy, age four, and their widowed mother. She could not remember much about the father who had died or the other family members they had left behind. She only remembered Grandma, standing at the railway station, crying and waving goodbye when they left on the train. Grandma had given Ella and Rudy each a little basket of cookies to eat later on the boat to America.

"When Mama got married again, along came baby Anna, and all my wishes came true," Ella said. "Not only did I have a new sister, but Rudy and I got a new dad."

Anna purred with delight as Ella spun her tale, and soon the room grew quiet. Ella knew the younger kids had drifted off to sleep. Smiling down at the tow-headed girl asleep in her arms, Ella toyed lovingly with the soft curls framing Anna's angelic little face.

"You never need to be afraid, little sister," she whispered. "I promise I will always take care of you."

Reaching over to the bedside stand, she shut down the lantern's flame and settled in to sleep.

True to promise, Ella was like a guardian angel to Anna throughout their youth. Despite her young age, Ella already had grown-up responsibilities, baking and cooking for the hired help right alongside her mother. Life was difficult on the untamed, dry farmland, but she always kept close watch over her younger sister.

Anna had been barely three when Ella took her to visit the shepherd's camp, nestled in the shade of the aspen trees near the foothills. When the girls arrived, newborn lambs were scampering all about, romping in the sunshine. The scent of freshly baked cookies filled the air. The sheepherder's wife had seen them coming and was delighted to have company, especially children. The girls had a wonderful visit.

A few days later, Anna decided it was time for more cookies. The sun was not yet high in the sky when she headed off, alone, for the shepherd's camp. She toddled along, stumbling now and again, as she followed any path she came to. The tall sagebrush had many animal trails leading through it, but to Anna they were simply trails leading to cookies. Soon, the day became hot and Anna grew tired. Lying down in a shadow, she soon fell fast asleep.

Back at the ranch, Ella realized Anna was missing. She ran through the house searching every possible hiding place, then dashed through the yard and down to the corrals and outbuildings, screaming Anna's name. Mama heard and came running, demanding to know where Anna was.

"She was with me one minute, Mama, and now she is gone. I have searched everywhere," Ella sobbed.

Mama rang the iron dinner bell, sounding the alarm that would call in the farmhands. For hours, everyone searched for the child but with no success. As night approached, a pall of fear settled over them. They all knew the dangers of the land, especially for young children. Huge rattlesnakes were everywhere, as were coyotes and cougars.

Ella was inconsolable, blaming herself for being so careless. She had promised to keep Anna safe and she had failed. It was all her fault. She perched herself atop a stone wall near the windmill, buried her face in her arms, and prayed desperately for Anna's safe return.

It was nearly dark when her stepfather rode back to the house and reported that he, too, had failed to find his little daughter. Just then, he spotted a cowboy riding toward him through the horse-high sagebrush; in his arms he held the plump and happy toddler.

"Praise the Lord!" her father cried out. "Where was she? We've been searching for hours."

"She was sleeping next to a deer trail down by the spring," the cowboy answered. "My horse shied, and when I looked down, there she was, sound asleep."

With a collective sigh of relief, the world soon returned to normal. Ella, however, made Anna promise her over and over that she'd never go anywhere without her again.

As the girls grew older, their school and work activities drew them into different directions. Only their evening hours were spent together around the big coal stove, where they stitched away at handwork that would go to fill their hope chests. Ella, of course, was the first to marry, moving away to a home of her own. It was a sad time for Anna; she missed her sister terribly. When it was Anna's turn to marry, she moved even farther away. Letters became the sisters' only means of contact.

In due time, both women became mothers. Ella's husband died young, leaving her with three daughters. Anna's marriage failed, leaving her with four children. And the two sisters went on with their separate lives, working and raising their children.

Late one fall with winter just ahead, Anna underwent major surgery. With her children grown and living far away, she worried how she would manage by herself during recuperation. As she lay in the hospital bed, fretting her circumstances, the door opened and Ella walked in.

"What a surprise!" Anna exclaimed, spontaneously reaching out her arms to embrace her older sister. "What are you doing here?"

"You need someone to take care of you," Ella said, squeezing her hands. "Remember, I promised to do that."

For several weeks, Anna stayed at Ella's home, recovering under her care. They sat close together, crocheting doilies and sharing memories. They talked of the good times and the bad, about the happy but hard days of childhood. When it came time for Anna to return home, both women wept as they hugged goodbye. The time had passed too quickly. And time marched on.

The hallway of the nursing home was bustling with noise and chatter when Anna arrived. She moved slowly down the narrow, sterile hallway, searching for a familiar face. Only yesterday, she had spoken with Ella's children, who had insisted she not waste her time visiting Ella. The Alzheimer's was too advanced. Ella did not know anyone anymore, not even her children. Still, Anna had come.

A nurse pointed to a room with the door slightly ajar. Anna peeked inside. Ella was sitting there in her favorite armchair, her eyes closed and her head slightly tilted. Her hair was unkempt and scruffy, her face pale and drawn. On the dresser a bouquet of flowers sat amongst photographs of people Ella no longer knew. The place was strangely quiet and disturbingly unfamiliar, a distant room pretending to be a home.

Anna slipped quietly into a chair close to Ella. She reached out and covered her sister's cold hands with her own. Ella's eyes opened slowly and searched until they found Anna.

"Hello, Ella. Do you know who I am?" Anna asked.

"You are my sister, Anna," Ella replied softly.

"Yes, I'm your sister. How are you feeling?"

"Not so well. I have a terrible headache."

"Would you like me to rub your shoulders?"

"Yes, please," Ella whispered weakly.

With gentle hands, Anna massaged the tightened muscles on Ella's neck, pleased at her sister's sighs of relief as the pain in her shoulders and head eased a bit.

"Oh, that feels good," she told Anna, before her eyes drifted shut again.

A few moments later Ella's eyes opened suddenly. "Where am I?" she asked, bewildered.

"You are in a nursing home. You have been very sick," Anna replied.

"Who are you?"

"I'm your sister. I heard you weren't feeling well, so I came to see you," Anna replied, blinking back the tears as her heart was breaking.

"Do I know you?" Ella questioned simply.

"I'm your sister," Anna repeated gently, tears trickling down her cheeks.

"I'm afraid," said Ella, her own tears starting. "I'm so afraid."

Anna reached out and held her sister in her arms. "I'm afraid, too," she told Ella. "But don't worry; I will stay with you."

"What is your name?" Ella asked again.

"Don't you know who I am, Ella?" Anna asked, sitting down. She looked deep into Ella's confused and tired eyes.

Ella studied Anna's face for a moment and then smiled sweetly. "I know you. You are my sister, Anna."

Anna's head drooped as she wept. Gently, she covered Ella's hands protectively with her own and nestled her head onto Ella's shoulder.

"Rest now, Ella," she whispered. "I'm here, and I promise to watch over you. You don't need to be afraid anymore. Just close your eyes. Your sister is here."

—*Jean Davidson*

# My Main Maid

My sister, Karen, and I are about as polar opposite as you can get. I'm athletic; she's not. She's a smoker; I'm an avid nonsmoker. I shop at Ann Taylor; she's more of a T-shirt and leggings kind of gal. Although we both have long hair, hers is blond and curly, while mine is brunette and straight. At twenty-four, she was married, with three kids. When I was twenty-four, I was out clubbing every night.

As different as we are, though, we've always loved each other and shared a close friendship. We may go weeks or even months without talking, but when we do we just take up wherever we left off the last time. That's a beautiful thing.

Which brings me to a special time in my life about four years ago, when I met and quickly fell in love with a wonderful man. It was a crazy, magical time, and Gary completely swept me off my feet. The romance moved pretty swiftly, and before I knew it, I had a rock on my finger.

Given my past dating history, my friends and family were stunned when I made my engagement announcement. The only one not surprised by my engagement was my sister. She'd known from the beginning of the relationship that I was deeply in love, and she was thrilled that I was getting married and settling down.

No sooner was Gary up off bended knee than I was poring through bridal magazines, attending bridal extravaganza conventions, and shopping for the perfect dress. I immediately went into overdrive, plotting and planning the wedding of my dreams. Then it hit me. *Out of my bevy of beautiful girlfriends, how would I be able to choose the bridesmaids?* I'd been in no less than twelve weddings over the previous five years and had a closet full of ugly bridesmaid dresses to prove it. No way did I want twelve bridesmaids. That much, I knew for sure.

I began to slowly and meticulously weed through the unsuspecting ladies, like a sniper wiping out her prey. Haven't spoken to her in two years. Delete. She was a real wench the last time I saw her. Delete. She always tries to one-up me. Delete. She made a move on my ex-boyfriend. Delete. So I continued the process until I'd pared down my list to a respectable five bridesmaids, including my sister.

I knew I wanted Karen to be in the wedding; that

was never in question. She had been there for me through the painful breakup of my last relationship, and we had grown closer since I'd moved back to Texas two months prior to meeting my husband. In fact, she actually drove the U-Haul that had brought me back from Phoenix. The two of us spent two full days on the road with all of my possessions and my cat stuffed into the small truck. But that's another story.

As I looked at the five names left on my list, it dawned on me that I should ask my sister to be my maid of honor. The maid of honor is, after all, the one that really counts. She's the one who plans your bachelorette party, helps you get dressed on the big day, holds your bouquet while you're saying your vows, has an extra Kleenex handy in case you get a little choked up, and straightens your train when you're walking down the aisle. She's your "main maid," so to speak.

Yup, that should be Karen, I decided. No doubt about it.

I picked up the phone to make the call, happy with my decision to appoint my big sister to the coveted position.

"I have a favor to ask you," I said.

"Sure," she said. "What can I help you with?"

"I can't seem to decide which of the girls I should ask to be my maid of honor," I said coyly. "Any suggestions?"

"Hmm," she said, trying to come up with some

sisterly advice. "Which one do you really want standing up there with you?"

"Well, that's easy." I hesitated, building up for the dramatic climax. "There's really only one who fits the bill."

"Who's that?" she questioned.

"You!" I laughed out loud, fully expecting her to join me, but was met with only silence. "Hello?" I said, somewhat confused. "Karen, are you there?"

"Yes," she finally whispered. "I'm here."

"Well, did you hear me?" I'd been expecting a laugh, a squeal, a giggle, a gasp of joy—some kind of jubilant response. "Will you be my maid of honor?"

"Are you sure?" she said.

"What do you mean, silly? Of course, I'm sure."

"You have so many friends," she said. "Why would you want me?"

"Yeah, I have lots of friends, and I'm sure any of them would be thrilled to be my maid of honor," I said. "But I only have one sister, and I want her up there with me on the most important day of my life."

"But I figured you'd want your best friend to do it," she said.

"I do," I said. "That's why I'm asking you."

—Susan Lynn Perry

# Trading Places

Sisters. I have two. But it wasn't always like this.

At six, I was a happy-go-lucky only child, fully enjoying the undivided attention of my parents and grandparents. I suppose I had just about anything a kid could want, except for those wonderful full-time friends, otherwise known as siblings, who can stay and play on the swings with you long after the neighbor kids are called home for supper. Yes, I dreamed of having a brother or sister like most of my friends had. Actually, I rather preferred to have a sister, since boys, as all six-year-old girls well know, have "cooties."

My prayers were answered. My sister Laurie arrived a few months before my seventh birthday and my sister Sheri a few weeks before my ninth. They entered the world as most babies do: small, helpless, noisy, and wet. Though I remember being amazed at the whole process, I was disappointed to discover that they weren't exactly the permanent playmates I'd had in mind. On top of their uselessness on the playground, their many needs reduced significantly my center-of-attention status in our household, something I had not considered.

Even so, I marveled at their sweet, soft perfection and the way they smiled when I walked into the room. I learned to feed them, dress them, and bathe them. I fell completely in love with them. They were my living, breathing dolls.

Around the time my youngest sister, Sheri, turned one, our lives turned upside down. Our parents embarked upon a drawn-out, nasty separation followed by a painful divorce. The story was sadly typical: man leaves wife and children for younger woman.

Long, stressful working hours, maxed-out credit cards, and heartbreak turned our once-sweet and available housewife/mother into a devastated, angry, and frightened working single mom. During this time, our mother could barely get out of bed in the morning, much less care for the every need and whim of her three daughters. Fortunately (or perhaps unfortunately) for my little sisters, they had me, their "junior mother," to fill in the gaps. I became my sisters' keeper.

Each day I would dash home from school so I could be there when they got off the bus. I helped them with their homework and cooked their dinner. I taught them how to color in the lines, how to ride a bike, the best way to load a dishwasher, and which music was cool. As they grew, my sisters began to resent my controlling influence on their lives.

My middle sister, Laurie, responded by quietly listening to and seemingly agreeing with everything big sis had to say. She developed a kind of calm acquiescence and moved through her life never straying from the straight and narrow. My sister Sheri reacted with outright defiance. When I went away to college, Laurie and Sheri chose completely different paths during their adolescent years. Laurie excelled in ways I'd never imagined. Sheri rebelled, first by skipping school and then with alcohol and drugs, and eventually landed in jail.

Meanwhile, I, finally feeling free from family responsibilities, went wild. I meandered from party to party, boyfriend to boyfriend, and major to major, searching desperately for direction in my life. Amazingly, after four years of college, I found myself with a great boyfriend, a degree, and a good job. Still, I spent my twenties unsettled and searching. I moved from job to job and city to city, and eventually I even left my great boyfriend, only to find myself lost again.

When I turned thirty, I got the urge to leave everything behind and live abroad for a year or so. But I worried my plan was just another escape.

A call to Laurie sealed my fate. Laurie had become a successful, responsible, and levelheaded young lady. In fact, she had become everything I had yearned to be since my departure from my role of mini-mom so many years before.

"Guess what I'm going to do," I said. "I'm going to leave my job, sell my car, put everything I own into storage, move to Europe, get a master's degree in something that has nothing to do with my career, and learn to speak French."

I expected, almost wanted, sensible, practical Laurie to talk me out of it.

"What a great idea," she said. "Can I come too?"

Our two-year European adventure helped us get to know one another again, not as big sis and little sis, but as equals and friends. Her gentle ways helped me to calm down. A technology whiz, she showed me the ins and outs of the computer. In our many travels, her mathematical mind resolved currency confusions and her amazing patience unraveled how to get from A to B in cities where we couldn't read a word. Most of all, Laurie taught me that I don't always have to be the big sister, always right and always in control. She taught me to let go and live life, one day at a time.

I stayed on in Europe and met and married the man of my dreams, Alain. Our son, Max, was born in the summertime. A first-time mother at the age of thirty-seven, I hadn't even changed a diaper since the last time I'd changed Sheri's diapers what seemed like a lifetime ago. I realized that all my years as a single, confused yuppie had not prepared me at all for the challenges of motherhood.

That December, my husband and I took Max home to meet my family for Christmas. The long trip took its toll on him. When we arrived in Florida, he was feverish for the first time in his young life and would not stop crying. I panicked. My youngest sister, Sheri, who over the years had found the courage to overcome her difficult start and had pulled her life together, was now an accomplished mother of two. When Sheri arrived, she took one look at Max and me and quickly took control of the situation.

With her arsenal of baby knowledge and easy-going manner, she had us both calm and comfortable in no time. During our holiday visit, she shared her motherly secrets and experiences with me. And we laughed at how the tables had turned.

Yes, I've learned a lot from my little sisters.

—*Donna Reay-van Strydonck*

 Double Sisters

I am the only child of an only child. I don't even have any paternal aunts. Nevertheless, I do have two sisters, and what's more, they are my double sisters.

They became my stepsisters when my dad married their mom. My parents' divorce had been traumatic for me, so news of the marriage was kept from me at first; Dad wasn't sure how I'd react. Because of the extra consideration I was given, I became "Queen Nancy" to Dotty and Wanda—not exactly providing a solid foundation for a sisterly relationship. Still, they tolerated me and eventually included me. Although I lived with my mom, circumstances brought us together frequently. As teenage girls will do, we talked about boys a lot. Dotty and Wanda just couldn't get why I wanted to talk about Teddy. How could I possibly be interested in their brother? You see, in addition to two daughters, Dad's new wife had a teenage son, upon whom I immediately developed a crush. I knew he liked me, too, because we overheard a conversation he'd had with his cousins. I remember us three girls standing on the other side of the partition, stifling laughter as we eavesdropped.

I never did get over my crush, and when we were twenty years old, Ted and I got married. Dotty and Wanda both participated in our wedding. And my stepsisters became my sisters-in-law—my double sisters.

I have learned, however, that a sisterly relationship doesn't necessarily happen because of the marriage of parents or even marriage to a sibling. It doesn't automatically occur even when siblings have the same biological parents. Just as love is a decision, so is sisterhood. It is the result of many acts of love, large and small, performed for one another. Girls are brought together by circumstances, but it is love, laughter, forgiveness, shared joys and sorrows that make sisters.

We shared the greatest sorrow of all—death—even before Ted and I got married, when my stepmom was killed in an automobile accident. A drunk driver crashed into the passenger side of the car in which she was riding. She lingered for several days, never regaining consciousness, and then slipped away, silently and forever. The shock of such an unexpected and unnecessary death caused us to hold on to each other tightly.

But that grip loosened as we each married and Dad remarried. We seemed to go our separate directions. Children came. Life was busy and full, and one day we looked up and it had been years since we had seen each other. I wish I could say it was I who initiated the contact, but it was Dotty who decided to be my sister.

"Hey, little sister, what are you doing the Saturday before Christmas?"

"Getting ready for it," I sighed. "There's always so much to do."

"Well, you'll just have to find another time to get ready," she announced. "We're all getting together at my house. We should see each other at least once a year."

Somewhat wryly, I realized I had missed Dotty and her directness. It would be good to see her again, but at the same time I panicked. I really did need the weekend to finish my last-minute Christmas preparations. I was both pleased and annoyed at the same time. Ted bought into the idea pretty quickly, but the kids were less than pleased. To be honest, they didn't know their aunts, uncles, and cousins very well.

I made one of my better decisions that year when I, too, decided to be a sister. Thus began a tradition of Christmas celebrations with our extended family that continues today and always brings much laughter and teasing. You never know what you're going to get in the white elephant Christmas exchange. Ted came home with two pink flamingos once.

But one family tradition wasn't enough for the intrepid Dotty Jo.

"Let's get together, just us sisters," she suggested.

"And do what?" I asked, my practical side asserting itself.

"Sit in your hot tub, gossip, and drink wine," Wanda proposed. The twinkle in her eye made Dotty and I laugh.

"Let's do it," I agreed.

So began a series of sister get-togethers and road trips, where we laughed and cried and teased and shared. On the third year of the sister trips, Wanda and I collaborated on a "get you" for Dotty. She had ragged on us pretty heavily at Christmas about the gray in our hair, while hers remained a lovely shade of red. We were well aware that Dotty and Ms. Clairol pooled their resources to achieve this color, so we decided to become redheads, too. The night before we were to meet Dotty, we spent the entire evening in the bathroom, applying rinse-out dye. It was worth the effort when we saw the look on Dotty's face as we waltzed into the restaurant where she was waiting for us. She had the last laugh, though. With the heat, Wanda and I began to sweat; the dye trickled down our necks and faces, and we quickly became red striped.

In between our "sister traditions," we checked on one another, kept up with each other's kids, sent birthday cards, shared our troubles, and were there for each other. When Ted had back surgery, Dotty and Wanda drove 200 miles to wait with me, and then together we celebrated the successful outcome. Once, when I was in a situation in which Dotty thought I might be taken advantage of, she showed up to protect me.

The strength of our solidarity as sisters and as a family was further demonstrated when Wanda's daughter got married. Many of us contributed to that special day. The wedding occurred on a gentle spring day in a grove of trees on Dotty's country property. Wildflowers graced the meadow, wind chimes sang in the air, and ribbons danced charmingly from the trees. God provided the wildflowers; the chimes and ribbons were courtesy of Wanda's daughter-in-law. The bride arrived riding in my convertible, driven by a chauffeur, my son. Ted, a deacon, witnessed the marriage. Wanda's son read Scripture; her grandchildren were flower girl and ring bearer. Dotty's son recorded it all with photographs. Then, of course, we celebrated at a reception, where the succulent barbecue was prepared by Dotty's son-in-law. My granddaughter caught the bride's bouquet. Even though she was only nine, we plan on filling her future wedding with family love, too.

Especially meaningful was Dotty and Wanda's support when my dad reached old age and needed special

244 ~ A Cup of Comfort for Sisters

care and love. They, of course, had no obligation, since he had remarried. I had no blood siblings to rely on, but I had my double sisters. They were there for his birthday celebrations and simply to visit. They provided transportation and phone calls, and perhaps most important, they lent me their ears and their shoulders. Dad was, to put it mildly, ornery in his old age.

As Dotty, Wanda, and I have grown older, we've often commiserated about the aches and pains of aging and the loss of certain abilities, not the least of which is memory. Wanda swears this joke was conceived with us in mind:

> Three very old sisters (Dotty, Wanda, and Nancy) lived together.
> One day the oldest (Dotty) drew a bath, and as she put one foot in the tub, she paused and called downstairs, "Am I getting in or out of the tub?"
> The middle sister (Nancy) started up the stairs to help and then paused and called downstairs, "Was I going up or coming down?"
> The youngest sister (Wanda) muttered, "I guess I'll have to help. I hope I never get that forgetful," and knocked on wood. Then she called upstairs, "I'll be there as soon as I see who's at the door."

One of the things I appreciate most about my sisters is their sense of humor. Ted and I achieved a lifelong dream and traveled to Paris, France. We brought back many stories, one of which depicted Ted, the deacon, being ejected from a cathedral because he took video pictures. Actually, he was asked nicely to leave the area, but the story grew with the telling. We arrived at Wanda's house shortly after our return, only to find that my sisters had induced the entire family to wear paper sacks over their heads, signifying their mortification and embarrassment at the deacon's expulsion. As the shamed wife, I was kindly offered a paper sack also.

Before I had sisters, I'd longed for siblings. I was lonely and expected to act like a miniature adult. It was so much fun to have other kids in my family. Yet, I didn't immediately fit in, partially because of my "Queen Nancy" status. In adulthood, I came to appreciate the full meaning of sisterhood. During childhood, my relationship with my sisters progressed from tolerated to partial inclusion. As adults, we progressed from estrangement to casual relationship, to tentative trust, and finally to complete caring and sharing. This was graphically demonstrated on one of the sister trips, when Wanda showed up with three T-shirts. Dotty's read, "Oldest Sister"; mine read, "Younger Sister"; and Wanda's read, "Youngest Sister." There I was, snuggled nicely in the middle.

Early on in the sister trips, we began collecting Christmas ornaments to remind us of our good times. Then, we began bringing ornaments back from individual trips as gifts for each other. Finally, we started exchanging ornaments at Christmas. Together we probably have enough to decorate the tree at Rockefeller Plaza. This year Wanda broke the custom. Instead, she got each of us, including herself, a picture of three little girls with their arms around each other. The caption reads:

> *We may not have it all together, but together we have it all.*

Looking directly at me, Wanda said, "We may not have been together when we were that age, but it sure seems as though we were."

We certainly are now.

—Nancy Baker

# Nudges and Lollies

My sister has moved away to the other side of the country. She has found herself a good job and a good husband; she is doing well. I am at university. I am spending all my money on my education. I am missing out on all the little things. And it is the little things I am missing the most.

I get home from university on a Friday afternoon. I throw down my bag of books and begin to cook my dinner: spaghetti on toast. Most of my dinners are spaghetti or baked beans or noodles. A university student knows these are the cheapest meals there are. I think about the weekend ahead. I have reading and assignments to do. I can't think of much to look forward to.

As I am eating my spaghetti there is a knock on the door. The lady next door hands me a parcel. It arrived while I was out, and she kept it safe for me. It is lumpy and bumpy, and it rattles. After prodding it for a while I choose to open it. I peek inside and see a packet of lollies. I grab them out. Then I grab out another packet. Then another. Then another. The smile on my face is pure radiance. I smile more as I think about how silly I must look. Surely only five-year-olds get this much joy out of a few packets of lollies. The parcel also contains a note from my sister: "Keep studying, sweetie. And don't forget to brush your teeth."

This simple thing makes me far happier than is rational. I mix all the lollies together, put them in a big jar, and place it on my desk. As I study, I reach in and grab myself a lolly every now and again. Somehow this simple thing keeps a smile on my face all night long. As the words on the page in front of me blur, I reach in and grab a lolly. As I start to tell myself this is too much work and I should give up, I reach in and grab a lolly.

Every week from then on I receive my little package of lollies. How did she know such a simple thing would somehow make me so much happier? I guess that is why she is my best friend as well as my sister.

My last year of university is dragging on. All the enthusiasm I felt in the first year has slowly drained away over the second and third and now I feel none of it. I have spent almost four years working hard toward a career. I have thought about that career endless times. I have thought about it so much that I have filled myself with self-doubt. I worry that after all this I won't be able to do the job. I won't be any good at it. I won't be a success. All this work will be for nothing. I tell my sister how I am feeling. She tells me I can do it, that I will be successful. I listen to her and tell her she is right, but I don't really believe it. And she knows it.

The next week I am sitting in my living room. Consumed by fear of failure, I have stopped studying completely. It is a defense mechanism of mine. At least then, if I fail, I can blame it on not studying rather than on not being smart or talented enough. Plus, failing will delay the arrival of the time when I actually have to get a job and prove myself, when I'll have to find the courage to test whether the last four years have been a waste of time. I am sitting at home watching television. I should be at university, but I have given myself the week off. I hear the sound of the postman. I rush out to the mailbox. I hope he has my weekly ration of lollies. With not going to classes, I have finished off all I had in the first two days of the week. The postman hands me a large yellow envelope. It is about the size a certificate comes in. I am not expecting anything. I rush inside and tear it open. I pull out a laminated sheet of paper. I read it through and then laugh. It is a table of contents page of one of my favorite magazines. Listed there is a feature article with my name under it: "'Finding the Nerve to Face Your Fears,' by Isobel Michelle" (my pen name). I smile and then giggle. I ring my sister immediately.

"You did this for me?" I ask her, as soon as she picks up.

"It is to remind you where you are going," she tells me, "and that you will make it as a writer."

"How did you do this?" I ask.

"I just scanned the page in and made some changes," she tells me. "You know you will make it."

I tell her how much of a thrill I get just by looking at my name there in print. It is everything I am working for, and she has made it seem real. Better than that, I *feel* it, almost as if it is real. I feel the thrill of being published, and I remember what all this study is for. My laminated poster goes up behind my desk.

In the months to come I receive more. One envelope contains a masthead of another of my favorite magazines with my name listed on the masthead at the top, as the editor. Another contains a front cover of a novel with me as the author. My favorite is a certificate that reads, "Isobel Michelle is hereby awarded a Pulitzer Prize for . . ." The background to the certificate is a family of dancing pens, holding hands and apparently doing the cancan. I am sure the Pulitzer looks nothing like this, but the thought was there. The dream is there. And I hold on to that dream. Thanks to my sister, I find myself unable to let it go.

—*Shelley Ann Wake*

Leaping Year Sisters

My sister's birthday is one day before mine.

"The only reason you two weren't born on the same day is because there was a leap year between nineteen fifty-eight and nineteen sixty-three," our father told us.

"Did you hear that?" I squealed. "There's a leaping year between our birthdays!"

"It's *leap* year, not leap*ing* year, you dork," my sister muttered under her breath.

"It just proves that I'm biologically accurate," our father would holler with glee when he was drunk.

"How can he say he's biologically accurate when we don't even have the same mother?" my sister asked me when she was ten years old.

"We don't have the same mommy?" I asked, stunned. I was only five, and this was new information to me. "Who is your mommy?"

She turned and stared at me with slitted eyes. "You're too young to understand."

"Is my sister adopted?" I asked Mom later that day.

A shadow passed over her face. "I'll tell you when you're older," she said.

Over the years I picked up bits and pieces of the truth from my parents' fights. Everyone but me knew who my sister's mother was, and they all seemed terribly angry with her.

My sister was treated like an outcast, the product of our father's brief and disastrous first marriage. In response, she shied away from my nearly constant attempts to be a sister to her. The only way I could be a part of her life was by going to church with her. When she rose early on Sundays to get ready to go, I was right behind her, tailing her like a puppy.

We always rode to church in the backseat of our father's smelly car. He would move his unwashed fishing net from the backseat to the trunk minutes before our departure. The horn would blare under our bathroom window. My sister would look at me in the mirror and roll her eyes.

"Do you think we can talk him into taking Mom's car?" I would ask, desperate to be helpful.

"No," she'd blurt out.

Then she'd check her lipstick one more time and pick up her purse to go downstairs. I followed, watching her waist-length hair swish like a horse's mane down her back.

"Please," my mother would plead in the driveway, "can't you take my car? What in the world do people think?"

"They don't think anything," Dad would say, waving us forward. "Get in, we're late."

The scent would hit us as soon as we opened the car door, the pungent odor exacerbated by the scorching Florida heat.

"At least run the air conditioner," Mom would call as we pulled off.

Dad would turn to look at us from the driver's seat. "Roll down the windows, girls, let her air out."

We would comply, grateful for the hot but fresh air that wafted in. We held down our hair with both hands as we made the blessedly short drive to the church.

One year earlier my sister had joined our tiny Baptist church by walking to the pulpit at the end of the service during the final hymn. I was shocked by her courage to walk down that long aisle and stand alone in front of all those adults, declaring her intention to become a member of the congregation. I was equally impressed that she did it in a dress that smelled like fish.

Two years later she ran away from home.

"I wish we were born on the same day," I said to

her once, when I was too young to understand her pain.

"Why?" she asked, her voice sharp as the blade of a knife. "So they can totally forget about my birthday instead of just ignoring it the way they do now?"

I started to protest, but she walked away from me, shaking her head.

The day I turned thirteen I went shopping with my mother to select a gift. My sister's birthday the day before had gone unrecognized. When we got home all of her belongings were gone.

"She's run away," Dad announced, his face stricken.

Mom and I drove to the house where we knew she had run, but she refused to come to the door.

"Why has she embarrassed us like this?" my parents asked each other.

I wanted to scream that it was because of the way they treated her, because her life was so inconsequential to them that they failed to acknowledge even the day of her birth every year. Instead, I went to the room I had shared with my sister and crawled into her bed.

I imagined that she had gone to California to find her mother. I dreamed that she would find her and live happily ever after. Her mother would love her and celebrate her birthday every August, come rain or shine. There would be cake and ice cream, hats, clowns, maybe even dancing dogs. I consoled myself that her life was perfect now that she had found her mommy.

I didn't hear from her again until I got a phone call from her two years later.

"How are you?" I asked, cordial and reserved, having grown up in twenty-four months.

"I'm living on the beach," she said, her voice loaded with weariness.

"You mean you aren't in California?"

She chuckled, and my heart ached. I hadn't realized how much I'd missed her.

"No, silly, I've been here all the time."

My parents had never told me. After she left, her name was never mentioned again, as if she had never existed.

"So, you never found your mother?"

"Oh, I found her all right."

The next day she came for me and took me to her house on the beach. The Gulf of Mexico swept nearly against her back door in long watery fingers as we sat inside drinking iced tea.

"So," I asked, swallowing my nervousness, "what about your mother?"

"Oh, her," she said, turning to gaze out of the back window, a gesture that seemed to put miles between us. "She wasn't what I expected her to be."

"What was she?" I asked. A million possibilities crossed my mind, none of them pretty.

"She was someone who wasn't cut out to be a mom. That's why she let Dad have me when they split up."

That was the moment I understood the pain she had shouldered all her life.

"And me?" I asked, setting my glass down so she wouldn't see my hand shake. "Am I cut out to be a sister?"

A sad smile lifted her cheeks.

"Yes," she said.

"Even though we never celebrated your birthday?"

"Even though."

I moved to sit by her on the couch, and she extended her hand with the pinkie finger jutting out at an angle.

"We're leaping year sisters, remember?" she asked.

"Leaping year sisters!" I exclaimed as I hooked my pinkie into hers.

We shook once, hard, a definitive action that sealed our union.

"Leaping year sisters forever!" she cried out to the ceiling, laughing.

—*Kelly L. Stone*

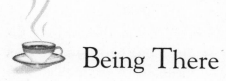# Being There

I was barely three years old on her wedding day. I wore a lacy pink party dress, and my Easter bonnet was perched atop my head, but it wasn't Easter. In place of tinted eggs, the basket clasped in my arms was filled with flower petals, which I'd been carefully instructed to sprinkle in front of me as I walked slowly up the aisle in time to the music.

Oh, that aisle. It had worked perfectly in rehearsal, but, as they say, that was yesterday. Today, the aisle stretched out for miles. The preacher and some other guys I barely knew were tiny penguins at the far end. A white carpet veiled the seemingly infinite path, lighting it up like an airport runway. And I was the pilot, responsible for the lives of everyone behind me—my sister, her friends, our father. I could barely see my mom, way down in front, twisted in her seat and craning her neck to watch my perfect three-point landing. What would she think if I crashed and wrecked everything?

To make matters worse, my mother was not the only one staring in my direction. The pews on either side of the runway—I mean, aisle—were filled with gaudily dressed aunts and uncles and grandmothers, overperfumed friends of the family, and snot-nosed cousins poking out their tongues and waiting (hoping) for me to screw up. I took one last look, and I made my decision.

"I'm not going," I said. And I didn't.

Of course, my sister got married that afternoon, anyway. And she's still married all these years later, so I guess my cold feet didn't do too much damage. Still, I wonder what it must have been like for that seventeen-year-old in her white wedding gown, trying desperately to control her own cold feet while contending with a stubborn little sister bent on ruining what should have been the happiest day of the big sister's life.

At the time, I was doing what seemed best. Best for me, at least, and when you're three, that's all that matters. In retrospect, I realize I was a tad selfish. After all, this was the person who had cried real tears when she first laid eyes on me and didn't see the dimples that should have marked us as sisters. This was the girl who had clapped her hands gleefully a few months later when I smiled for the first time, revealing at last those tiny indentations in both chubby cheeks.

Even after the wedding day fiasco, there were no hard feelings. She showed me how to color inside the lines. She taught me to make chocolate-chip cookies and eat them neatly, so I wouldn't get caught spoiling my supper. And it was my sister—not my mother—who told me where babies come from. I was only five at the time, but she was nineteen and suddenly fatter than Santa Claus. What a relief when she told me her bulging tummy eventually would become my nephew or niece. All in all, I figure I owe her a lot. Especially after reneging on my flower girl engagement.

The years flew by, the way years do, and my nephew became two and then three. And a niece was thrown in for good measure. Both my sister and I moved away from our hometown, only I traveled west while she went east. The white wedding gown faded to yellow, and the flower petals dried and crumbled and blew away. We all got older, the way people do.

One of us, though, didn't get much older. Instead, he got very sick.

He would have been my friend even if he hadn't been my nephew. And he was the son of the woman who would have been my friend even if she hadn't been my sister. He called me on the fourteenth of March to tell me he was dying. Five months to the day later, he was gone. If you think that years fly by, how fast must five lousy months be? Yet, they were the longest months of my life, of all our lives. Especially the life of that woman whose belly swelled to contain him and who surely taught him to color and eat cookies and where babies come from, just as she had with me.

When she learned that her son would quit the Earth before her, she left her home in New Mexico and traveled west again to care for him.

"I saw you into this life," she whispered to him on the phone. "And if you have to go, I'll be the one to see you out of it."

My friend—my sister's son—called me from Phoenix, anxious and upset.

"She's not that well herself," he told me. Which was true. "She'll be miserable in this heat," he moaned. Also true. "She'll worry herself sick if she's here taking care of me."

"Too true, sweetie. But what do you suppose she'd be doing if she stayed home?"

She didn't stay home. She went to Phoenix and cared for her dying son. I visited as often as I could, but it was never often enough. Never long enough. And through all my visits, all the shared love and memories and laughter in his house couldn't disguise the fact that he was getting weaker day by day. If I could have saved him by going back and becoming that three-year-old coward in the not-Easter bonnet,

I would have done it. I would have marched up that bright white aisle in my pink-lemonade dress, and I would have flung those petals into the air and up to the stained glass windows and even into the faces of those sweaty aunts and gassy uncles and bratty cousins. I would have done it, even if I would have crashed and burned. If I could have saved him by sacrificing myself, I swear I would have done it.

But, of course, I couldn't. I could not go back in time and change even one moment of that long-ago summer wedding day. Now, it was another summer, another heat-drenched afternoon in the Arizona desert. And my nephew kept getting sicker and weaker, and eventually he died. And my other friend—the one who loved my dimples and shared cookies with me and told me about the birds and bees—was left behind to grieve.

Our parents drove the family to my nephew's too-empty house in their van. On the way to the mortuary, my sister and I huddled together on the way-in-back seat.

"I feel like my heart is going to explode and burst right out of my chest," she sobbed.

"I know," I said. "I'm going to hold you, really tight, to make sure that doesn't happen. That's why I'm here."

Suddenly, I knew why that beautiful bride had put up with that spoiled brat on her wedding day.

Why she'd been so patient and loving and understanding all those years. Why she'd taken me under her wing, taken the time to teach me all she knew about crayons and chocolate-chip cookies, and, yes, even sex. And about the big important stuff, too—like love and life. And death.

I guess my sister must have known all those years ago that there'd be some kind of payoff if she waited long enough. But she couldn't have known the price she'd have to pay in return.

So why am I telling you all this? To assuage my guilt? Atone for the sin of breaking my vow to my sister by refusing to play flower girl at her wedding? Offer up my confession and be absolved—presto!—on the spot? Well, when you're raised by Methodists and your sins include everything from pinochle to prom dates, you learn to take your absolution wherever you can find it.

I remember a different wedding. It was yet another summer in that same arid place—*is it always summer there?*—and I was the one in the wedding gown. The ring bearer was a three-year-old, as I had once been. And if he'd balked at the last minute, refused to budge, turned and fled through the double doors and out into the street, I would have been devastated.

But not this toddler. He strutted up the aisle in his miniature tux and two tiny black shoes, as though he'd been piloting blushing brides all his life. No crashing and burning, no veering off-course, no turbulence of any kind. My special day went off without a hitch. Which was wonderful, of course, but scary, too. Because I knew I hadn't paid yet. Hadn't said the Hail Marys and Our Fathers that would allow me to be forgiven for the sins of misguided fear and unabashed self-interest I had committed on that other wedding day, even if they were perpetrated by my less-reasoned three-year-old self.

That debt was to remain outstanding for another twenty years. Then came that miserable March 14, followed much too soon by that horrible August 14. Crouched beside my sister on the way-in-back seat of our dad's van, I knew that her heart was about to explode and burst right out of her chest. So I held her really tight to make sure that didn't happen. That's why I'm here.

—*JayCe Crawford*

# Kerry's Portrait

"Remember, draw what you see, not what you think you see," my sister Kerry reminds me.

"I know that. Be quiet." I bite my lower lip, groan, and erase the same line for the fifth time. If I erase any more, the paper will be permanently smeared.

I sit and study my sister as she reclines on the other side of the porch swing, unconcerned by my frustration, painting the toenails on her right foot bright red. As I watch, she tucks a strand of chestnut hair behind her petite shell-pink ear. Her hair possesses chameleon-like qualities. From Orphan Annie curly to wand-straight, from little-girl long to pixie short, from raven to towhead, Kerry's hairstyles have marked the decades. As a little girl I played hairdresser with her fried and frosted eighties-style locks. I spritzed her hair and styled it, wrangled it into pigtails and yanked it into braids as she tried not to scream. When the pain got to be too much, she held up a cracked yellow hand mirror to admire my handiwork, kissed me on the cheek, and promised not to ruin her hairdo for at least a week. I try to capture the transient quality of my sister's hair on paper, but it looks straight and flat and slightly frizzy from the Florida humidity.

A tiny red ant starts to trespass on my drawing, moving slowly but surely over my sister's head. Not wanting my handiwork to be permanently smeared with bug guts, I try to gently flick the ant onto the redbrick floor. The ant disappears. Where did it go? Did I get it off the paper? Is it still on my finger? I can't see the ant, but it feels like something's crawling in my hair. I drop my pencil and swat at my head and shake my hair, and get up and swing my head around in circles, running my fingers through my hair at the same time. My sister starts to laugh.

"Kerry, it's not funny. I think there's something in my hair."

"Let me see," my sister commands.

I walk over to her and bend my head down. She separates my hair slowly with her fingers, and I feel like I'm back in third grade being examined for lice. I shiver in disgust.

"I don't see anything," she says.

I grab my pencil and my artwork, which I scattered across the porch in my frantic bug raid, and sit back down on the swing; but by now I've started to itch all over. Finally, I try to start drawing again. I look at Kerry, and she's looking at me, smiling. I scowl at her, and grinning, she goes back to painting her toenails.

When she smiles, my sister's almond-shaped eyes narrow to slits and crinkle in the corners. Her eyes bring back some of my earliest memories. Being nine years older, Kerry loved to tease her baby sister. I can still picture her big face close to my small one, her dove-gray eyes narrowed and twinkling mischievously as she blew on my hair or tickled me or tried to kiss me. Right now, though, her eyes are wide and silent as she concentrates, and I can't quite capture them on paper. I shape them and shade them until the paper starts to stain and the air smells rubbery like the eraser, but they still look cold and lifeless. I study the picture closely, so closely my eyes start to blur. Then, I look up and notice the menacing gray clouds slowly darkening the sky.

"Kerry, please go turn on the porch light. It's getting hard for me to see."

She caps her polish, stands up, and grabs at her baggy blue sweatpants, which have fallen downward, displaying a peek of her white granny panties and the dimple at the top of her butt. A moment later, the yellow halogen porch light flickers to life, instantly disturbing an assorted collection of moths and other small insects.

My sister leans back against the swing, crosses her arms against her chest, and closes her eyes. Pesky mosquitoes buzz by her head, and I can picture one of them accidentally sticking to the greasy petroleum jelly my sister smears on her full lips to keep them hydrated. I laugh inwardly as I imagine the poor bug immobilized and buzzing shrilly as it fights for its life on my sister's sticky mouth. Truthfully, Kerry's perfect lips make me jealous. But it's hard to stay jealous of lips like my sister's, lips that are always kissing my cheek or pulled back in a grin. When my sister smiles, old ladies pat her face, children hug her legs, and men fall to her feet. I can't seem to capture the perfection of my sister's lips with a pencil. They appear too large or too small, too broad or too narrow, too pouty or too perky. None of the lips look like Kerry's. Nothing seems quite right, and a drop of sweat suddenly drips from my forehead, smudging her long, straight nose.

The sky looks truly ominous now, full of deep dark clouds, and the heavy humidity feels like a warm, wet woolen blanket. The paper starts to wrinkle under my sweaty hand. In frustration, I begin to rapidly sketch my sister's dimpled chin and her long, elegant neck. With just a few strokes, I try to capture her strong shoulders and soft, comfortable arms. Then, I move to my sister's hands, the hands of an artist. I struggle to draw her fingers, which are long and supple and surprisingly strong but end up looking spidery and delicate. My sister is unique, as unique as her bright purple fingernails, and the banal, awkward lines of my portrait don't convey how special she is, how perfect. I have failed. I was never meant to be an artist.

With a deep sigh I throw my drawing to the ground and collapse back against the swing.

Kerry opens her eyes and asks cheerfully, "Are you finished?"

"Yes. It sucks."

"Let me see."

I shake my head.

"Come on, bubba. I bet it's great."

I lean over, grab the paper, and shove it at her.

She grabs it from me and immediately says, "Wow, that's really good. That really looks like me." After a moment, she adds excitedly, "You really got my eyes and my hair and the shape of my face . . . and my lips, you really got them. That even looks like my nose. Noses are really hard to do."

My sister's enthusiasm is infectious. I can't help but believe her.

She hands me my drawing, kisses my cheek, and says, "You did so well. Now, sign it and give it to me. I'm going to hang it up in my room."

My sister has kept everything I have ever made for her since kindergarten. No matter how simple or how ugly it is, she carefully packs it away.

I sign my drawing, hand it back to my sister, and stretch out on the swing with one foot on the ground and one foot stretched across my sister's lap. We sit with our eyes closed, swinging together. We smell the rain, like mold and metal, sweet and redolent in the moist air. We listen to the heavy silence, broken only by our slow, steady breathing and the low, rhythmic groan of the swing.

Suddenly, a bright flash of lightning bursts behind my closed eyelids, immediately followed by thunder so loud it shakes the ground and rattles the cement. My sister and I scream, and side by side, we scramble toward the door and squeeze inside the house, bursting into the air-conditioning and light. We lock the door as if that will protect us from the electric storm. Then, we stand there listening, each breathing heavily, each with our hair mussed, waiting for the lightning to strike again. Finally, I look at her, and she turns to look at me, and we laugh as we stand shoulder to shoulder, happy and warm and safe from the storm.

—*Brittany Melson*

# Placid Drive

When I was five years old my family moved to Placid Drive, smack in the middle of what my sister called "Nowhere, America." There were only a few houses along our dirt road— rusty farm homes with needle-straight grass and scratchy fences. My sister and I rode past these houses every day, ringing our bicycle bells with loud *brrrrringsss*, popping wheelies with a jerk of our handlebars, and taunting each other back and forth with, "I'm gonna beat you." We raced to the finish, a yellow construction sign that read "No Outlet." She usually did beat me—her ten-speed over my banana seat—and she would laugh smugly all the way to the end of Placid, the only road that led to the Ulmstead barn, where the neighborhood horses lived.

From the first time she heard the sound of hooves clomping, my sister vowed to have a horse of her own.

She spent weeks wallpapering her bedroom walls with pictures of ponies, and she doodled stick-figure drawings on notebooks. She placed monthly *Horse Lover* magazines in the bathroom reading rack, where my parents couldn't miss them. When Mom and Dad pretended not to notice, she threw a fit, begging and pleading, promising and praying, warming and buttering, until somehow, my parents bit. After her tantrums and tears, Jean Renee got her pony. She named it "Bunny."

The Ulmstead barn with its neat red trim looked like a picture in one of those home and garden magazines my mother read. But instead of being shiny white with a fresh slap of paint and a green garden backdrop, this barn was the color of sawdust souring in the sun. From the outside, it looked barely tended to, with weeds winding around the silo and ivy choking at the roof. The paddock doors outside the barn creaked open and slammed shut, over and over again all day long, at the whim of whatever humid breeze happened to pass. On the inside, the barn was dark and damp and smelled like leather.

Walking into the barn was entering a world unseen. No matter the time of day, it took a few moments before my eyes adjusted to the dimness. The first time I went in, I barely made out the long hallway of hidden stalls and ceiling rafters. As the doors slammed shut, a flourish of fly-paper strips waved in the wind, textured with tiny winged corpses frozen on sticky film. Oily white paint peeled from the walls and doorways, curling in ways that called to me.

The passageway was always still and soundless except for the scuff of my shoes. To my side were silhouettes of discarded saddles and rusty tack, and bright blue brushes tangled with hair. Barn cats slinked out from their hiding places, gray and matted and mice-fed, covered in mites and crying. Pellets of grain scattered the floor, and horse shoes donned doorways—always face up, for luck.

The hollow hallway led to the loft. While my sister hauled grain and pitched manure, I hid upstairs among straw bales and squirrel droppings. I imagined I was a runaway, storing supplies of carrots and trough water to make it through the winter. They'll never find me, I would think, smiling to myself. I can live here forever.

The hayloft wasn't the only secret place in the barn, as I soon discovered. I stole away to shadowy horse stalls and clanged steel gates behind me. Once inside the stall, I fantasized about being in a carnival or the circus. Here, I could be a clown on stilts or, my favorite, one of those long-legged, high-diving beauties.

Standing tall on an overturned water bucket—my twenty-story diving board—I peered through the steel rails and clicked my tongue. "Ladies and gentleman, horses everywhere . . ." I grinned into the dusty stall, delighting in echoes railing above me. Horses shuffled in their shoes with brown egg-eyes blinking and dumbstruck. I lifted my arms wide and rounded my chest, and with one last look, I plunged—leaping forward, landing headfirst into my hay mountain, luckily missing buried manure below.

"She did it, everybody!" I marveled to the horses around me. Rolling in the scratchy bale, I basked in my death-defying feat and listened to echoes of the barn: floors creaking, voices muffling, beasts clamoring inside steel cages.

I stared up into the dimness of the barn—no lights except what filtered in from a few faraway windows. Yellow dust floated down and up and all around, lifting and spinning inside a current of air made visible by the light. There was no sound except for horses chewing, grinding their teeth. Dust caught in my throat, and my eyes began to itch. Inside my box, inside my head, I was behind closed doors, but free.

Then I heard that voice. My sister's voice.

"Come on!" Irritated at my existence, at her responsibility.

I waited, quiet, wondering if she would find me.

"*Now!*" She spoke through clenched teeth, startling me. "I said come *on!*"

I sighed, knowing I could no longer be a trapeze artist, a runaway, a long-legged anyone. As soon as I heard her calling, kid sister was all I was. "Kiddo," she called me.

It was time to go.

Back at home, when my parents told my sister and me to "play nicely," we pretended we were in the movies. She loved Clint Eastwood westerns and strutted around in a cowboy hat and chaps. Between our kitchen and foyer swung two white-paneled saloon doors, just like the Old West. One lazy afternoon, my sister stormed through the doors with both hands on her guns and sauntered up to the breakfast bar, spurs clicking at each step.

"Barkeep," she snarled with a side grin, "fix me a stiff one."

I poured us two shots of lemonade in Dixie cups, which we downed in one gulp, wincing like we were drinking the hard stuff. We nodded at each other with squinty eyes and whispered, "Smooth." This was the funniest thing we'd ever heard. We fell over ourselves laughing at one another, as we launched into an unspoken game of who could make the goofiest face and the best Western wisecrack.

This went on for a good while, but then my sister got serious.

"This town ain't big enough for the both of us," she growled.

I giggled again, but she didn't laugh. She pulled the water guns from her pockets and started firing at me, square in the eyes.

"Aw, no," I screamed and turned to run, but in my haste I tripped, smacking hard onto linoleum. Pain pulsed on the inside of my bottom lip. I put my hand to my mouth and felt my chin wet. When I saw the blood, I started to cry, gasping for my breath as she stood over me.

"You wait till Mom gets home," I threatened her through my tears.

Then I'd see her squirm with fear. She knew that if I told on her, she would be in big trouble.

I always told on her.

Days when we didn't go to the barn, I ran away without going anywhere. I hid in closets or under beds, in corners and behind doors. Sometimes I snuck around like a secret agent spy, collecting clues to some unknown mystery.

I crept inside my sister's room and searched for her diary or other concealed goods. This was dangerous work and took daring on my part. It could be done only when she was home, because she locked her door behind her when she left. I had to wait until just the right moment—right before she was about to leave the house, when she scurried between her room and the bathroom, arm-deep in curling irons and eyeliner and makeup mirrors. Her distraction was my opportunity.

As soon as her head was in a fog of Aqua Net hairspray, I slipped inside her door and dove underneath the bed. Safe! I lay there on the cool hardwood floor, making my mark in the frosting of dust babies, and waited. Sometimes more than an hour would pass before she finally left, clicking the door behind her. Once my mom called for me, but, of course, I couldn't come out. I remained at my post until the enemy left and I was free to start my assignment.

When she did leave, her room was mine. I searched through her notebooks; I thrashed through her clothes. I was an expert spy, a secret agent who had infiltrated unknown territory. Every five minutes or so, I darted my eyes back and forth and spoke into my wristwatch: "Agent M here. Mission under way." I kept my voice low, clearing my throat a couple of times for effect. "Subject has left the building. Over." I continued my search, humming the music from television's *Get Smart*.

I learned a lot about my sister through these spy efforts. I found stashed Parliament cigarettes, empty Bartles and James bottles. Juicy letters to boys I didn't know. Diary entries about losing virginity.

Virginity?

I wondered about that one. I didn't know she had virginity in the first place. Later, I asked my mom about it.

"Hey, Mom, what's virginity?"

She paused in picking out shell fragments from a bowl of backfin crabmeat and wiped her mealy hands on a paper towel. "Where did you hear that word?" She looked me square in the eyes beyond her glasses, scowling.

"Um, a magazine," I stammered. Suddenly realizing this might be bad, I covered, "*Seventeen* magazine."

"Oh," she said and looked away. Long pause. "Well, what it means is . . ." She went back to picking crab, fingers buried deep in stringy white meat. "A virgin," she said, clearing her throat, "is . . . someone . . . who isn't . . . married."

I was thoroughly confused.

"A virgin means not married?" I got the feeling I should drop it, but couldn't. Not until I got to the bottom of this. "So, then, if you lose virginity, it means you're married? Like, to a husband?"

"Sort of, yeah." My mom sighed. "Go play now."

And with that I guessed that my sister must be secretly married. I couldn't believe it. First, she shaves her legs and now this. Did my parents know? They couldn't. Surely I would have heard about it before now. Shocked by my expert spy work, I breathed into my mood ring, low and slow and sure of myself.

Mission accomplished.

When my sister left home, we sold the horse. She was eighteen, after all. She had a boyfriend (who, according to what I had learned, was actually her husband, for all I knew), and she no longer needed a horse.

We drove down to the barn—the four of us, the last time as a family—to say goodbye to Bunny. While my parents talked to the new owners, I wandered around the Ulmstead barn, picking up stones, kicking at driveway dirt. I knew I wouldn't have reason to come there again. My hayloft was gone, all of my hiding places exposed. In its place was a fancy reception hall where they held weddings and Super Bowl parties. I knew I would never see an invitation.

I felt sorry for myself until I saw my sister petting Bunny for the last time and crying. Her shoulders sank silently, her back turned to my parents so they wouldn't see. She looked small to me for the first time, small for being a big sister. Small and alone and afraid to move on—not just from the barn and Bunny. But from us—her family, her childhood. I walked over to her and stood quietly, just slightly behind her. She never turned around to look at me, but I remained close enough so she would know I was there. Close enough so she would know that's where I would always be.

—Elaine C. Gast

# Wet and Naked

Throughout childhood my younger sister Allison and I bathed together in our parents' oversized claw-foot tub. We lathered one another's hair in mock shampoo commercials. We wrung drenched washcloths over each other, plastering hair to foreheads and laughing so hard water ran into our mouths. Once we were in the tub, Mom had trouble getting us out.

In adulthood, an autoimmune disorder robbed Allison of her health and agility. The disease transformed her from a slim, willowy dancer to an inflexible, fragile Olive Oyl.

One autumn, an odd compilation of ailments plagued her. Her left breast was infected and swollen. She had an abscess on her right buttock and a lesion on her underarm that refused to heal. The threads in the seams of her clothing tore open her fragile skin.

She arrived at my kitchen door clutching Epsom salts and a bottle of tea tree oil.

"I've come to use your tub," she said and handed me her things. "I have to soak my butt."

My parents still had their extra-long, antique tub, but as her body defied her, she chose to recline in my smaller version. Once again, we shared a tub, this time out of necessity, not for fun.

As she poured her ingredients under the steamy faucet, I adjusted the water. She looked at me with the fatigue that soldiers must feel after a long battle in the trenches.

"I want to keep this under control so they don't have to pack it," she said with a weak smile.

"Soak as long as you need," I said, forcing a return grin. But my stomach tightened.

The year before I had held her hand as she screamed and wept in the emergency room. The nurse packed the abscess on her knee, poking lengths of gauze into a hole so deep I could see beneath her skin to the smooth cartilage below.

"I'll be outside raking leaves," I said. "Just let yourself out when you're finished."

An hour later, I walked into the bathroom, smelling like leaves and cool air. I jumped when I saw Allison sprawled in the tub. She lifted her head and scowled at me as if I had put Jell-O in her bath instead of Epsom salts.

"Still here? I thought you'd be gone by now," I said, puzzled. "Isn't the water getting cold?"

"Yes, it is," she said through her clenched teeth. "In fact, it's been cool for a while now."

"Then why didn't you get out?"

"Because I can't bend my knees," she growled.

Her condition changed daily, and I hadn't considered her knees stiffening. Horrified at my thoughtlessness, I flung my shirt on the floor, plunged my arms into the tepid water, and tried to bend her knees for her. She screamed in pain, and I withdrew my arms like the pain was my own.

I slid my hands up her legs toward her bottom, to hoist her onto her feet.

"My abscess!" she screamed in warning.

"Okay," I said, yanking my hands back, holding them in the air like a surrendering soldier. "What if I lift you from behind?"

Shoes, socks, and jeans fell beside my shirt. I stepped into the cooling water. After many aborted attempts, I was soaked, the floor was covered in puddles, and Allison was still stuck.

Wiping oily drips from my face, I held my head in frustration. Buttocks, bosom, armpit—all too inflamed to touch. I slumped on the edge of the tub and looked her up and down.

"Where can I touch you?" I asked.

She looked sheepish. "I don't know."

"I'll call Mom."

When Mom arrived we mapped a strategy, listing viable body parts like inventory clerks. Somehow, as the flesh had melted from her bones, Allison had become a series of parts and afflictions: "the abscess," "the lesion," "her knees." But her whole person was stuck in my tub.

Mom stripped down, too. Her full bosom and round belly complemented the trapped stick figure.

"How did I make a daughter like you?" she asked, staring at her own plump thighs.

Mom lifted Allison's thighs, bending so low her breasts touched the water. I stood behind Allison while she braced her back against me. In an awkward dance, we lifted and rotated until Allison's long legs dangled over the tub's edge and I was flattened against the wall. Slippery flesh pressed together, I longed for the innocence and health of our youth.

As I disentangled myself from the shower curtain, Allison stood up in halting stages, like an arthritic old woman. She was twenty-nine.

Wet, naked, and now laughing, we toweled off. Three women in a tiny bathroom, the walls echoing the laughter, muffling the pain.

While Mom mopped water from her cleavage, I mopped the puddles from the floor. As children we'd left great pools after our splashing competition to see who could make the highest tidal wave. Feet flat on either side of the faucets, knees bent and full of potential energy, we'd snap our legs straight. Our tiny bodies shot though the water like torpedoes, forcing a wave up the tub's sloped back. Being bigger, I always won the contest with Allison but lost the battle with Mom. I had to mop up the overflow of our tsunami match.

Now, as I blotted the oily water with a towel, I wished it were as easy to wash the disease from my sister's body, to catch it neatly in a towel and toss it away. I'd have given all my childhood memories to wipe the disorder from her, to wring out the poison and realign her immune system like a freshly smoothed sheet.

The last puddle wiped up, I wandered into the kitchen. Allison was stretched over the kitchen counter, stark naked, bottom in the air. My mother, her bra and underwear speckled with oily water, was hunched forward and staring intently at an angry welt on the exposed posterior.

Brow wrinkled in concentration and nose inches from Allison's right cheek, Mom raised her head and looked at me. "Do you have a flashlight?" she asked.

The absurdity of the situation struck us with a tidal wave of laughter. We leaned against each other and howled, heads back, eyes closed. Allison's laugh swept me back to the days of dripping hair and mouthfuls of soapy water. Her distinct, strong guffaw defied her dwindling muscles. She was strong and whole in that laugh, and I scrunched my eyes tightly, as if clamped eyelids could keep us safe and happy in the past.

As laughter ebbed I gulped air like I'd been drowning in the memories. Hoots rolled into chuckles and came to rest in gentle smiles. Still grinning, I pulled the flashlight from the junk drawer and snapped it crisply into my mother's extended palm like an operating room nurse. She resumed her inspection.

"It's healing nicely," she said.

After saying our goodbyes, I returned to the bathroom. The oil and salts formed an uneven loop around the porcelain. The tub ring, like my family circle, was fragile but unbroken.

—Charmian Christie

# Prom Night

I hated my sister. I adored my sister. I stole her socks and her makeup, and I would have stolen her boyfriend if I could have, except I was only ten when she started dating him. His name was Julio, and he was tall and lanky, with eyes that filled up the top third of his face. He was a runner, and so my sixteen-year-old sister, Carol, began to run, and then, of course, I started running too.

Julio gave her things, things I coveted, things like old T-shirts and sneakers, and their first Christmas together he gave her a wooden jewelry box he made in shop. It was the most beautiful thing I'd ever seen—all smooth with varnish, a little drawer that made the nicest squeak when it was opened, and lined with red felt inside. Red being the color of love, I knew it was a secret message from him to her.

Ah, love! She was so lucky to be in love with

someone who loved her back. I was no stranger to love; after all, my half of our room was lined with posters of Donny Osmond. We were going to get married someday, just as soon as I bumped into him and he fell instantly in love. Until then, however, the closest I got to real love between a boy and a girl was watching Carol and Julio.

For some reason, probably my mother, when I pleaded with my sister to take me along when she went off with Julio, she grudgingly said yes. This was the same sister who usually walked so fast when I followed along with her and her friends that I had to run to keep up. She'd always hated having me along. Yet, when Julio came along, I found myself in her royal presence more often. It helped that he liked me. The two of us would get going on some silly thing and we would crack my sister up.

Soon I was going along with Carol to Julio's track meets, sitting in the bleachers under a scratchy army blanket that smelled of gasoline, sipping watery White Castle hot chocolate. When the summer months rolled around, I'd squeeze into his Camaro with them and a couple of other teenagers and we'd head for the Jersey shore. I didn't have much of a life outside of tagging along with my sister. Oh, sure, I had my friends and school, but nothing was near as glamorous as my sister who worked at the diner, managed to get her ears pierced despite my parents' protests, and wore the most marvelous blue eye shadow.

It's pretty clear I idolized my big sister, but it's also true that we were worst enemies. Even though I got to go along on many adventures, there were many more that I was barred from. Prom, for example.

Julio and Carol went to junior prom together. That was hard on me, the prom being what I considered a "ball." Carol not only got to dress up in a full-length red gown, get her hair done at the beauty parlor, and go with a boy who should have been my date, but when he showed up he was wearing a matching red cummerbund and carrying a wrist corsage. What could be more romantic than a wrist corsage? As my mother snapped pictures of them in front of our apartment building, where Julio's freshly waxed car was parked, I watched with envy boiling in my veins. Carol looked like a princess, and what was I? Cinderella without the fairy godmother. I could stand it no longer and ran to our bedroom crying. Throwing myself on my bed, I sobbed into my pillow.

Carol came in a few minutes later to see what was wrong. I refused to talk to her.

"Aren't you going to wish me a good time?" she asked.

"No! I hope you die!" I squawked out.

My sister wasn't expecting this. It was one thing to say mean and evil things in the heat of battle, but this venom was unexpected and unprovoked. I heard her gasp, then heard her platform shoes thump away from me. The bedroom door closed and all that was left was the smell of her perfume, Love's Baby Soft.

A few minutes later I heard my mother call to them as they left. "Be careful. There'll be a lot of drunks on the road; make sure one of them isn't you."

I cried a bit more, then got up and did what always made me feel better. I rifled through Carol's stuff. Usually, I made a point of trying not to let her know I'd been there. But that night I didn't care. I began in her underwear drawer, looked at a handful of pictures she kept there of her and her friends. There was one of her and Julio, my Julio. I tore it in half and put the side with Carol back in her drawer and kept the one of him and put it under my pillow. She'd see what I'd done and there'd be a brawl, but I didn't care. I welcomed it.

My next stop was her makeup bag. I unzipped the floral pouch, and the scent of powders and creams tickled my nose. I removed a deep red lipstick and pressed it hard against my mouth, pursing my lips and then kissing my hand, wondering what it would be like to feel Julio's lips on my own. I closed my eyes, imagining it, and opened them suddenly when the image revealed him kissing my sister. I slammed the top on the lipstick without turning it down, squashing the creamy color with glee. Next was the blue eye shadow, her treasured blue eye shadow. I thickly applied it to my own lids, then a layer of black mascara, followed by her expensive blusher.

Finished with her makeup bag, I turned my attention to her half of our closet. She worked hard waiting tables and spent most of it on her wardrobe. I found a pink satin blouse and a pair of black velvet pants she'd worn on New Year's Eve. They were too big, the pants definitely too long, but a pair of black platform sling-backs took care of the length problem. Dressed, I admired myself in the mirror. I looked at least sixteen, I figured. Old enough for a boyfriend. Old enough to go to a prom.

I put on my eight-track of Donny Osmond and played "Puppy Love" while dancing with the teddy bear Julio had won for Carol at the carnival. I played the song over and over until I fell on my bed in sheer exhaustion from feeling sorry for myself. All that self-pity can tucker a girl out.

Sometime around one o'clock in the morning, I woke up. Carol's bed was empty. My overhead light was still on. A glance in our dresser mirror revealed a Halloween face. The lipstick was smeared, and the mascara and eye shadow had smudged so it looked like I had two black eyes. My big sister's clothes looked just that—big. I looked like some sort of sad little clown. I kicked off the shoes, peeled off her clothes, shoved them under my bed, and pulled on a nightgown. I went into the kitchen for a glass of water. My mother sat at the table, chain-smoking Kool cigarettes.

"I told her I wanted her home by midnight," she said. "What are you doing up? What's on your face?"

"Huh? Nothing," I said. Much to my amazement, my mother left it at that.

I filled a glass of water and sat down at the kitchen table with her. She didn't tell me to get back to bed. Something was definitely wrong here.

"She's probably having a good time and forgot what time it is," I said.

"I told them the later it gets the more dangerous the streets become. I know kids drink on prom night. Every year some kid gets killed. There, in the paper, the day after prom is their picture. Two young kids, dead because of a drunk driver."

A chill went down my spine as I remembered my last words to my sister. *I hope you die.* What if God had heard my wish? What if my sister was wrapped around a tree somewhere? I tried to take a sip of the water, but my throat had seemingly closed up. So, I just sat with my mother and listened to her inhale the cigarette smoke, then exhale. Every now and then she'd report the time: "one fifteen," "one thirty," "one forty-five." We waited, hoping my sister would walk in the door any minute. Praying that she and Julio wouldn't be the annual sacrifice of youth. Not my sister, God, not mine.

I thought of every mean thing I'd ever done. The time I got her in trouble for scraping soap in my eyes when she was working on an art project and I had stupidly lain on the rug at her feet. Mom had smacked her with a hair brush for that. It had been my fault. So many times, so many things, all my fault. Then I remembered the list of wicked things I'd done that night. The lipstick, the makeup, the picture. The picture I'd torn in half!

I got up, went to my bedroom, and retrieved Julio's torn picture from beneath my pillow. I found Carol's half. How could I do such a thing? I taped the two halves back together. I knew it was still obvious, but I was convinced that if I didn't tape that picture together I would be going to my sister's funeral. I only hoped it wasn't too late. I said another silent prayer: Please, please let her be all right. I didn't mean it, not any of it. Please, just let her come home.

Here's the weird thing. She did. Right then, at that moment, there was a turn of the lock and Carol clumped into the kitchen still wearing the corsage, albeit wilted, on her wrist. She also was holding a floral centerpiece and placed it in front of our mother on the table.

"Look what I won," she said as she went up and gave my mother a kiss.

For the second time that night, I started to cry, but this time I ran to my sister, who was again taken aback.

"What's with you?" she asked.

"I have no idea, but I'm going to bed. You're late, you know," my mother said sternly, but obviously relieved.

"I'm sorry, we—" Carol began, but Mom cut her off.

"Tell me in the morning. I want to hear all about it, but right now I'm beat," she said and kissed us on the heads.

Carol and I went to our bedroom, and as she removed her prom dress she told me all about the night's events. I knew there was going to be hell to pay when she realized what I'd done to her things, but I'd gladly pay the price. At that moment, my big sister was a celebrity and yet she was my sister. This golden girl was miraculously related to me, shared my bedroom, would share her life with me. I was so incredibly lucky, and though I often forgot that during the mere two more years we lived together before she moved away to college and then her own home, I knew it that early morning after prom.

Several years ago, Carol's best friend gave her a plaque that reads, "It's chance that makes sisters. It's hearts that make friends." Occasionally while growing up Carol and I were both friends and sisters. Today, we always are.

—*Kathy Coudle King*

# Moments

To this day I cannot descend into a basement without hearing my sister's voice: "No, really, this time I won't do it, I promise."

I don't know why I always thought "this" time would be different. Call it respect for her big-sister authority. Call it an abiding trust in her words. Call it not too bright. But like a loyal little lemming, I would go as I had gone a hundred times before . . . down the speckled linoleum stairs to the cold damp place where Mom did the laundry, Dad had his workshop, and monsters waited in the dark. Once we were deep inside the bowels of this mysterious world, I'd think to myself, *See? It's not so bad.* Right on cue, Marta would scream like a crazy person, run up the stairs like a track star, and turn off all the lights—leaving me alone in that dark scary place . . . again.

She read as fast as she ran. Marta would plow

through an entire book in the time it took me to get through a few short chapters. One summer our family went camping, and after a long day exploring the Lincoln Trail, I reclined inside the rented pop-up trailer with a book I'd purchased especially for the trip. It was the story of the beautiful antebellum Bella and the two men wooing her heart. I turned each page with tingling anticipation, wondering which one she would marry. Would it be Harry or George? The suspense was building. Suddenly, the light-weight camper door flew back on its hinges.

"Bella marries George!"

Marta's laugh faded as she ran away.

Every now and then, I tried to retaliate. Once, I decided to use the silent-sister treatment. Marta came into the room. I didn't look at her. She spoke to me. I didn't reply. She spoke again. Silence. Giddy with my newfound authority, I strutted across the room, reached for the *Highlights* magazine lying beside her chair, and gave her my snottiest who's-in-charge-now look.

"Are you not talking to me?" she asked with a hint of a smile.

I remained silently firm.

Then my sister said the words I will never forget: "If you don't talk to me, I'm going to tell Mom and Dad you don't love them."

I haven't stopped talking to her since.

Recently, I reminded my sister about these episodes. She pointed out that perhaps I needed to accept some responsibility for the repeating basement scenario, seeing as how I fell for it every single time despite the consistent, inevitable, could-it-be-more-obvious ending. She may have a point.

As for Bella and the fellas, Marta explained that she was bored and wanted to spend time with me. It worked. I never did finish reading the book, and I did have fun with her that vacation. She assures me it was a lousy story anyway.

When I repeated her words about not loving our parents, she looked shocked. "I said that? That's terrible." Then she grinned a little. "But it worked didn't it?"

Then her smile faded. "Was I a bad big sister?"

"No," I said, without hesitation. "You were a wonderful big sister. You still are."

"Are you sure?"

And so I told her about a few other moments I remember.

We had a cement driveway when we were kids, the kind that develops cracks after awhile. Every spring Dad filled the cracks with tar to keep them from growing wider. We loved to dig our bare toes in the sticky black goop. One day, as we felt the first drops of an afternoon downpour, Marta raced into the house and grabbed Dad's huge umbrella with the curved wooden handle. She carefully placed it over some especially thick tar, situated herself under the canopy, and pulled me in beside her. Safely shielded from the rain, we talked and laughed and picked at the warm tar until our nails were black. It wasn't much really, just a couple of sisters sitting under an umbrella, alone in the world and having the time of our lives. I'll never forget how good I felt that day.

I loved rain in the daytime, but thunderstorms at night terrified me. We slept in bunk beds then, Marta on top, me below. We had a real Michigan boomer one night, and I cried quietly into my pillow, as ashamed as I was afraid.

"Come on up here," she said.

She had never invited me to the grown-up top bunk before. As we lay on our tummies together high above the ground, she pulled back the curtain, revealing the storm. I listened fascinated as she described each strike.

"That's called scribble lightning," she said. "That's zigzag."

The storm eventually faded, and when I climbed down again, I was no longer afraid of something with a name.

In those days, Popsicles were the favorite summer snack. All over the neighborhood, sticky wooden sticks indicated where a kid and a Popsicle once had been. There were secret messages imprinted on those sticks.

I couldn't see them, but Marta assured me they were there, and she was the only one who could read the invisible clues. Each clue took us to another hiding place. We ran from the big rock next door to the willow tree in the front yard to the mailbox on the corner— searching for treasure. Often, it was a beautiful stone; sometimes, it was a penny. One time, it was an earring. Whatever it was, she always gave it to me.

When we were growing up, she was the active one, full of energy, always trying new things, taking hold of life with complete confidence. I plodded along with caution, deliberate, unsure of myself, afraid of nearly everything. We were as different as two sisters could be then. Somehow, we managed to grow together and find our common ground, sometimes pushing, sometimes pulling, but mostly side by side.

Today, we both live in a charming little town in the foothills of the Smoky Mountains. Marta teaches English as a second language to young children. I recently moved here after a twenty-five-year marketing career in Detroit. It's nice to be near my sister again. We spend a lot of time together, talking, laughing, and enjoying each other's company, sharing memorable moments like only sisters can. We even went into a neighbor's basement the other day. Marta stayed with me the whole time.

—*Mary Jane Chew*

Not Another Like Her

At seven, she'd already seen her parents divorce and graciously accepted a stepfather. At nine, she was hit by a car and lost a year relearning to walk. During those long months, she was trapped at home, watching her mother lose baby after baby. Adoption agencies told my parents that at their ages, they'd never be given an infant. Julie gave up her dream of being a big sister.

She turned eleven two months before I was born. I came to them unexpectedly, through word of mouth. A doctor knew a girl, another knew a family, and six months later on a Saturday morning I was bundled into a car and driven to my new home.

We were children of two working parents. They had the weekend to coo at me and Monday morning returned to work. My days were spent with babysitters, and each afternoon, Julie would rush home to take over the next shift.

At six months, I contracted scarlet fever and squalled to bring the roof down. Only one photo from that awful time remains: It is of my pale, exhausted twelve-year-old sister, asleep in a rocking chair, holding me. Her hands, huge and strong for a young girl, are tight around me even in sleep. My own chubby form is sprawled across her, my dark head nestled on her blond shoulder. I can't imagine a safer place.

When I was growing up, our parents seemed like ghostly entities on my periphery. My dad was never a challenge to me. Though my mother was the giver of "no's," she was easily ducked. My sister, on the other hand, had my number.

I was well known for my ferocious tantrums. My dad was known for plugging his ears and shouting, "Give the baby what she wants!"

It was Julie who rolled her eyes in disgust and made me set my room to right after I'd destroyed it in a fit of temper. It was my sister whose patience was tested time and again by my kicking, shrieking, and stomping.

When Julie landed a job working at the parks and recreation department, I hung from her belt loop, dragged along on aquarium and zoo adventures. I saw every movie made at the drive-in with my sister and from her learned to be a fabulously bad bowler. She was the queen of the "just because" banana split and the giver of the coolest birthday presents.

Throughout my childhood, Julie was always quietly behind me, watching over me, making certain I lacked for nothing. She bought my school clothes and made sure I was okay, really okay. I had no idea that all big sisters weren't so vigilant.

At seventeen, Julie moved into her own home. She would've taken me, had my parents allowed it. I cried and then went silent when they didn't.

I spent weekends with her. And she continued to "steal" me for fun stuff—shopping and trick-or-treating and trips to the lake.

As I grew, we had our arguments. At ten, I defied one of her rules, for the first and last time. Two years later, in a moment of hormonal teenage fury, we had the inevitable face-off. I screamed that she wasn't really my sister, she wasn't my real family, and I wasn't going to listen to her. Crushed, she told me what no one else had ever dared to voice: She had raised me when she was still a child. Had my "real" mother wanted to keep me, she could have. In tears, she told me she didn't deserve such words from me.

She was right. She was more than a sister. At eleven, she'd voluntarily shouldered the responsibilities of a grown woman. She'd cared for me selflessly, every single day of my life, and never once complained.

Julie walked away and left me sitting with the Irish setter she'd given me for my ninth birthday. I cried like I'd never cried before. She'd named my worst fear, the fear I had never voiced. She'd known all along and loved me anyway.

Somehow, the years passed. She had her own child when I turned fourteen, but I wasn't made of the same stuff as my sister and played no more of a role in my nephew's babyhood than would any other typically self-involved teenaged aunt. Like Julie, I, too, moved out of our parents' home when I was only seventeen.

Later that year, my sister developed cancer. Her son, Shane, was only three, and she told me before she entered the hospital that if anything happened to her, she expected me to watch over him. I balked at the thought and was too afraid of losing her to come near. Julie had surgery to remove the tumor, followed by hellish chemotherapy, and over the next year, slowly regained her strength.

As her health returned, I started borrowing Shane. I took him swimming, to the zoo, and to the beach. Now and again he'd spend the weekend with me.

When Julie got sick again, I was pregnant with my first child. As my baby grew inside me, any chance for another child was taken from her. Again, we feared Julie would leave us.

Six years later, we live 6,000 miles apart—she and her son in California, my children and I in Ireland. Our relationship could have drifted into an exchange of greeting cards in December. Yet, she was with me when my sons were born. We talk on the phone every other week. Next December, I'm bringing my boys home for Christmas.

Her boy spent last summer with us. We all know he's getting too old to hang out with his little cousins and aunt, but Shane has a soft heart, just like his mama.

Now, with children of my own, I realize Julie has never been given half the credit she deserves for taking care of me from the day I was born. Having done the rocking and walking, the bathing and feeding, the comforting and sleepless nights myself, as an adult, I'm awed at the burden she shouldered while still a child. I now understand the faith she'd placed in me when she asked me to watch over her son when she came close to leaving us. Could I have raised him as well as she raised me? Thankfully, we'll never know. What I do know is how fortunate I am that an eleven-year-old girl took me into her heart and took such loving care of me. How proud and grateful I am to call that remarkable woman-child my sister.

—Lori Alexander

 Just as Is

*S*tomp, stomp, stomp. Slam!

Classic sounds of my older sister Mari in her teens, in distress after a scolding, storming off and shutting her bedroom door behind her. Such passionate and dramatic behavior coming from someone so usually placid and easygoing as Mari always made me and my other two sisters laugh.

"There she goes again," we'd say.

More concerned about house damage, Mom would yell, "Stop that, Mari. You'll break the door."

That would set off another round of giggles.

None of us bothered to bring Mari tissues or offer any sisterly hugs of comfort. We all knew the ritual. Within minutes, Mari would come out, apologize to Mom and give her a hug, smile at the rest of us, and be back to her usual contented self as if nothing had happened. She'd plop down in front of the television to watch *Three's Company* or some other sitcom, laughing her head off.

"I wonder what she's in trouble for this time," one of us would say.

"Didn't do her homework," or "Didn't brush her hair," or "Knocked over a lamp," or "The usual," another would say.

Mari never seemed to do anything right. Careless, clumsy, and rather unkempt, she gave Mom many reasons to nag. Even when she wasn't at fault, she'd automatically get the blame because she seemed the likely culprit. Happy-go-lucky Mari rarely defended herself or held grudges, and that made her an easier target.

None of these occasions moved Mari to change. An early childhood illness had left her slower than she'd been, generally passive, and with an almost perpetually pleasant and affectionate demeanor. Although capable of doing many things, she simply lacked the ability and will to focus and to excel.

Eight years my senior, Mari had no special knowledge to share with me, no skills to teach me. Following my Mom's cue, I found myself finishing her sentences, correcting her speech, telling her how to groom herself properly, and warning her to watch where she was going so that she didn't bump into something or someone. She'd go along with my suggestion for a moment only, and then return to her usual unsophisticated, klutzy self.

I often felt embarrassed at having Mari as a sister. She needed fixing. It bothered me to hear her mispronounce things like "Bob's Bigs Boys." It bothered me to see food or lipstick on her front teeth. It bothered me when a silly joke would make her cackle with abandon, even in a quiet or somber setting. What bothered me most was that none of this seemed to bother her one bit.

Overweight, unstylish, and far from articulate, Mari didn't fit my ideal of an older sister, a female role model. Fortunately, I had two other older sisters who together seemed to fit the part well. One was an athletic and savvy go-getter. The other was creative, conscientious, and maternal. Mari didn't have much to contribute, and I just had to accept that.

After scraping through high school and half-heartedly taking some junior college courses, Mari found work and moved out on her own. Mari was living independently: what great news! But how painful it was to see how she lived. My first visit to her apartment became my last. Dirty clothes, crinkled magazines, candy wrappers, half-eaten food, and other trash covered the floor of her bedroom. You couldn't tiptoe across the room without stepping on things along the way. Her car was no different. A sticky layer of dust blanketed the dashboard and sides. Peep under the seats and you'd find a handful of loose change, old receipts, paper clips, gum wrappers, popcorn, and a whole assortment of other fallen munchies.

I said nothing to Mari. Mom was aware of Mari's mess, and I figured that if she couldn't pester Mari into cleaning up, I certainly couldn't. Besides, even amidst that chaos, Mari appeared the same: blithe and strangely content.

Years passed, and Mari remained Mari. She made little money, yet, for no special occasion, she would give generously to others, especially Mom—watches, jewelry, lunches. Being childlike herself, Mari especially adored our little nephew, who, in return, gave her the biggest hugs and granted her the title "Spoil Auntie." Mom would urge Mari to use her money on a haircut or a car wash, instead. But Mari continued to give, never expecting anything in return. Heck, she hardly ever stuck around long enough for a thank-you.

Then came the marriage proposal. Her very first boyfriend, John, was a giant of a man with a hearty sense of humor. He held a regular job, carried on intelligent conversations, and dressed in crisp, clean T-shirts and jeans. I remember trying to find faults in him because I couldn't identify his attraction to Mari. But somehow it had happened. In true fairy-tale fashion, the two exchanged vows under a gazebo at the Disneyland Hotel.

When my turn at the altar came around, Mari offered her help. Days before my wedding, I sat at the dinner table with my fiancé and Mari, organizing car-pools and figuring out other details. Among them was how to transport my wedding gown and veil. I ran through my options and realized that all were problematic.

"I know," Mari jumped in. "We can take them in my car."

"No," I said. "That won't work either."

"Why not?" she asked.

"I can't take my dress in your car," I snapped. "It will get dirty."

With no more discussion, I moved on. Mari looked saddened and hurt, but I had plans to make and lists to complete. Meanwhile, Mari continued to sit there, waiting to offer any help she could.

Months after we were married, my husband and I had a rare argument. I can't remember what about, but I do remember him accusing me of being mean sometimes.

"Mean?" I said. "Like when?"

That's when he brought up the day I'd snubbed Mari.

"Have you ever looked inside her car?" I defended myself. "There are all sorts of things growing in there."

By then, my husband had known Mari long enough to acknowledge that possibility. Still, his raised-eyebrow expression told me he wasn't convinced of my innocence.

"I was just being frank," I pressed my point.

"And Mari was just being nice, as usual." Then he brought out the double-barrel: logic. "Look, your dress was wrapped up. Nothing would have ruined it. You should have let her help you."

He was right. Mari would never have put me or anyone else down as I had her. While I often pointed out her faults, Mari always treated me with tolerance and respect. It suddenly occurred to me that Mari's attitude, behavior, and maturity level far exceeded mine. It had taken me years to see what her husband, John, had spotted straight away.

Not long ago when I was visiting Mom, Mari stopped by and left her car in the driveway for a few hours while she ran errands nearby. Mom and I dragged out the vacuum cleaner, gathered up rolls of paper towels and cleaning materials, and went to work. We wiped away the thick film from the windows and chiseled off food from the floor. We laughed as we examined some of the items we found in between and beneath the seats. When we were through, the car looked almost livable and, after excavating the litter of her life like an archeologist, I felt one step closer to my sister. When Mari returned, we handed her the loose change we'd salvaged from the front seats and some wrinkled slips of paper we weren't sure she'd want thrown out.

"You guys shouldn't have," Mari said in her usual cheerful tone. Then she laughed out loud and gave me her usual bear hug before picking up her keys and driving off.

Thinking back, I don't think she was particularly impressed with what we'd done. In fact, I don't think it made much of a difference to her one way or the other. She is, after all, completely content with her life, with herself, and with her family—just as is.

What greater lesson could an older sister give?

—*Ritz Imuta*

# Tell Your Story in the Next *Cup of Comfort*!

We hope you have enjoyed *A Cup of Comfort for Sisters* and that you will share it with all the special people in your life.

You won't want to miss our next heartwarming volumes, *A Cup of Comfort Devotional* and *A Cup of Comfort for Mothers & Sons*. Look for these new books in your favorite bookstores soon!

We're brewing up lots of other *Cup of Comfort* books, each filled to the brim with true stories that will touch your heart and soothe your soul. The inspiring tales included in these collections are written by everyday men and women, and we would love to include one of your stories in an upcoming edition of *A Cup of Comfort*.

Do you have a powerful story about an experience that dramatically changed or enhanced your life? A compelling story that can stir our emotions, make us think, and bring us hope? An inspiring story that reveals lessons of humility within a vividly told tale? Tell us your story!

Each *Cup of Comfort* contributor will receive a monetary fee, author credit, and a complimentary copy of the book. Just e-mail your submission of 1,000 to 2,000 words (one story per e-mail; no attachments, please) to:

*cupofcomfort@adamsmedia.com*

Or, if e-mail is unavailable to you, send it to:

A Cup of Comfort
Adams Media
57 Littlefield Street
Avon, MA 02322

You can submit as many stories as you'd like, for whichever volumes you'd like. Make sure to include your name, address, and other contact information and indicate for which volume you'd like your story to be considered. We also welcome your suggestions or stories for new *Cup of Comfort* themes.

For more information, please visit our Web site: *www.cupofcomfort.com.*

We look forward to sharing many more soothing *Cups of Comfort* with you!

# Contributors

**Lori Alexander** ("Not Another Like Her") is a freelance writer, "karate mom," environmental activist, and retired behavioralist. Born and raised in the United States, she now lives in Dublin, Ireland, with her husband, Brian, and two sons, Jeremy and Gavan.

**Dawn Allcot** ("A Plane Ticket, a Phone Call, and a Country Song") lives on Long Island, New York, with her husband and three cats. A freelance writer, she is a regular contributor to several magazines and Web sites, including *Church Production Sound, Sound & Communications, Paintball Sports International,* and N2Arts.com.

**Teresa Ambord** ("When Lightning Strikes") teaches career accounting at Lake College in Northern California. She lives with her teenage son, faithful dog, and two cats.

**Shirley Anderson Bahlmann** ("The Worst Babysitter in the Whole World") is the author of five published books. She grew up as one of six sisters (and has two brothers) and is now mother to six sons. Shirley works at home, fitting her writing around her active family.

**Nancy Baker** ("Double Sisters") resides in College Station, Texas, with her husband of forty-five years. Upon retirement, she pursued her lifelong love of writing and has been published in national magazines and anthologies. She directs the ministry to the sick program at her church and is a hospice volunteer.

**Nancy Bennett** ("Throwing My First Homer") lives in a small community on Vancouver Island, Canada. Since quitting her job two years ago to write full time, she hasn't looked back. She and her husband share three cats, a German shepherd, a chubby rabbit, the occasional bear, and two daughters.

**Virginia McGee Butler** ("The Problem with Paybacks"), a working writer and retired teacher, lives in Hattiesburg, Mississippi, with her husband and chief proofreader, Al. This first publication in an anthology features her original and most enduring fan club—her sisters, Beth Jones, Gwyn Pennebaker, and Ruth Page.

**Bobbi Carducci** ("Changing Currents") is a freelance writer living in northern Virginia. She and her husband, Mike, have a blended Irish/Italian family that brings endless inspiration and joy to their lives and her work. Mornings often find her in the hot tub, sipping tea as the sun rises over the Blue Ridge Mountains.

**P. Avice Carr** ("Sister Power") is a human tumbleweed. She has rolled through twenty-nine towns in North America, living and collecting stories. Today, she resides in Ontario, Canada. She is the mother of five daughters and the grandmother of eleven children.

**Mary Jane Chew** ("Moments") graduated from Purdue University with a bachelor of science in marketing and journalism. After working in the Detroit automotive marketing industry for twenty-five years, she moved to the foothills of the Great Smoky Mountains, where she sits today with her cat, Suki, admiring the scenery and pursuing a writing career.

**Rebecca C. Christensen** ("The Favor") and her husband, Jeff, after having moved twenty-seven times between Maryland, California, and New York, finally settled on beautiful Bainbridge Island, Washington, where they make their home. This is her first published story.

**Charmian Christie** ("Wet and Naked") is a writer from Guelph, Ontario, Canada. Her writing career spans instruction manuals, plays, training videos, essays, magazine articles, and short stories (fiction). In her spare time, Charmian does community theater, where she takes comfort in knowing she isn't as crazy as the characters she portrays.

**JayCe Crawford** ("Being There") lives in Los Angeles, California, where she is currently compiling a collection of travel stories. When not writing, she works in the music business and volunteers at the Los Angeles County Museum of Art. Her essay "The Road" is featured in the L.A. County Superior Court's juvenile intervention program.

**Barbara Davey** ("A Poet Lives Here") is an executive director at Christ Hospital in Jersey City, New Jersey, responsible for marketing, public relations, and fund-raising. Her writing has been published in several anthologies, including A

*Cup of Comfort.* A graduate of Seton Hall University, she holds bachelor's and master's degrees in English and education.

**Jean Davidson** ("Sure of You") lives in Pocatello, Idaho, where she is currently a full-time student at Idaho State University, studying whatever piques her interest. She is a wife, a mother of three grown children, and "Mee-Maw" to five grandchildren. Her greatest pleasures come from recording and bringing to light her family's stories.

**Margaret B. Davidson** ("Surviving Skylah"), born and raised in England, now lives in Fairport, New York, with her husband and cat. Retired from a paying job, she devotes her time to improving her writing, playing tennis and golf, and traveling. She and her sister chat daily by e-mail.

**Laura Deutsch** ("Psychic Sisters' Hotline") is a writer, writing coach, editor, and teacher based in Mill Valley, California. Her personal essays, news features, and travel and humor pieces have appeared in numerous periodicals, including the *New York Times*, *More*, *Mademoiselle*, and the *Schuster.* Her broadcasting experience includes work with public radio and public television.

**Karin Crompton DiMauro** ("Party Night, Excellent Night") lives in Niantic, Connecticut, with her husband, Mike, where they both work as reporters for *The Day* newspaper and as freelance writers. The couple has a penchant for adopting cats, practicing photography, rooting for the Yankees, and playing with their nieces and nephews.

**Laura S. Distelheim** ("My Sister, the Mother") received her J.D. degree from Harvard Law School. Her literary nonfiction has appeared in numerous journals and anthologies and has been nominated for *Best American Essays* and the Pushcart Prize. She lives in Highland Park, Illinois, not far from her sister and her nephew, Ethan, who is now a nine-year-old bundle of energy.

**Samantha Ducloux** ("Come What May") has published fiction and nonfiction under the names Samellyn Wood and Samantha Ducloux. She lives with her husband in Portland, Oregon. Her three children, six stepchildren, and their families give her immense pleasure, as does her frequent contact with her sister.

**Alice C. Facente** ("Bonded Through the Ages") was raised in a lively family of three sisters. She enjoys working as a visiting nurse at Ledyard Public Health Nursing Service in Connecticut and recently completed her master's degree at the University of Hartford. She and her husband, Brian, have two grown children.

**Elaine C. Gast** ("Placid Drive"), a freelance writer and yoga teacher based in Haiku, Hawaii, holds a master's degree in writing from Towson University. She has authored books for nonprofit organizations and published articles in national magazines and newsletters, and she currently writes for local newspapers on Maui.

**Shanna Bartlett Groves** ("Silly Little Prayer") is a

freelance writer specializing in articles about parenting and home improvement. She and her husband make their home near Kansas City, Kansas.

**Betsy O'Brien Harrison** ("The Promise") is a Pittsburgh, Pennsylvania–based freelance writer. Her work has appeared in national publications including *Whispers from Heaven*, *Teacher* magazine, and *Chocolate for a Teen's Dreams*. Happily married for twenty years, she is the mother of three.

**Ann Newton Holmes** ("A Fossil for Molly") is the coauthor of two coffee-table books on the glories of Rajasthan, India. Though Napa Valley, California, is home and "truly a place where God lingered," she spends two months in India each year researching Hindu architecture with her husband.

**Ritz Imuta** ("Just as Is"), a freelance writer who grew up on the West Coast, has also lived in Asia and Europe and now resides in Pennsylvania with her husband and two daughters.

**Marla Kiley** ("Till Death Do Us Part") lives in Denver, Colorado, with her husband and two sons. Her articles have appeared in numerous magazines and newspapers. When not at the computer or changing diapers, you can find her airing out her brain on a long walk.

**Kathy Coudle King** ("Prom Night") teaches writing and women's studies at the University of North Dakota.

318 ~ A Cup of Comfort for Sisters

Her first novel, *Wannabe*, about growing up in a Cuban-American community in New Jersey, was published in 2000. A playwright and aspiring screenwriter, she lives with her spouse and four children in Grand Forks, North Dakota.

**Jacquelyn A. Kuehn** ("Love Through Nine Bananas") lives with her family in the hills of Pennsylvania, where she works as a musician and writer. Banana Jane and her family live there, too, now occupying the oak sideboard. She is delighted to report that she and her sister Barb have completely reconciled.

**Angie Ledbetter** ("Hand in Hand") writes and cleans house in Baton Rouge, Louisiana. She and her twin sister, who live a few blocks apart, together write a joint humor/advice column and recently coauthored, with two friends, an inspirational book.

**Kathleen Brunson McNamara** ("Blue, of Course") is a health writer living in the San Francisco Bay area. She spends her spare time learning tai chi, stitching, restoring flea market finds, and gardening.

**Brittany Melson** ("Kerry's Portrait") is a senior at Florida Southern College in Lakeland, Florida, with a major in English and a minor in Spanish. She spends her mornings playing poker at the local senior center and her evenings reading old Harlequin romance novels.

**Anne Brownson Mize** ("Finding Tigers, Losing Janet"), child psychologist and creative writing instructor, resides in Seattle, Washington. Her writing appears in *Scent of Cedars: Promising Writers of the Pacific Northwest*, *The Christian Science Monitor*, and *The Sun* magazine. Having spent much of her life in Africa, her passions are wildlife and her Ethiopian daughter.

**Diana Parks** ("Tramps of the Neighborhood") is one of six sisters. She lives all over Atlanta, carpooling the four children she shares with their incredible father. When her fingers are not tapping the steering wheel, they are tapping out stories on the keys of her computer.

**Susan Lynn Perry** ("My Main Maid") manages a high-tech engineering firm by day and works on numerous writing projects at night. She is the author of two novels and is currently working on her first children's book. She lives in New Braunfels, Texas, with her husband, Gary, and son, Justin.

**Eve Powers** ("Houses of Gold") lives in Hawaii, where she recently relocated from Eugene, Oregon. Her work has appeared in numerous magazines and in the anthology *Scent of Cedars: Promising Writers of the Pacific Northwest*. She received a double first prize by the National League of American Pen Women for her stories "The Perfect Book" and "Visibility."

**Donna Reay-van Strydonck** ("Trading Places") lives in Belgium with her husband, Alain, and their two sons,

Max and Alex. She works as a public relations officer for the European Union in Brussels and holds degrees in communications and international relations. She loves traveling, spending time with friends, and playing hide-and-seek with her little boys.

**Tamekia Reece** ("Not Only My Sister") is a freelance writer residing in Houston, Texas. Her work has been published in *Black Enterprise, College Bound, Listen, The Next Step, Planned Parenthood, Pregnancy, Women's Health and Fitness,* and other magazines. She loves reading, traveling, and giving advice.

**Linda Today Robinson** ("The Magical Bond of Alexabeth") enjoyed a ten-year career in technical writing before giving it up to pursue creative writing. She lives in Minneapolis with her husband, Tim, and twin daughters, Elizabeth and Lexi.

**Julia Horst Schuster** ("Ah, Fruitcake!") is a columnist and book reviewer. Her stories have appeared in consumer and literary magazines. She is president of Emerald Coast Writers in Destin, Florida, and editor of the nonprofit group's annual literary journal, *SandScript: A Journal of Contemporary Writing.*

**Bluma Schwarz** ("Three-Part Harmony") is a semiretired mental health counselor and freelance writer residing in Florida. At age sixty-nine, she published her first story in *Iowa Woman.* Her stories have since appeared in numerous publications, including *Potpourri, Potomac Review, AIM,* and several volumes of *A Cup of Comfort.*

**Terry Miller Shannon** ("Tales of the Lawn Ranger") mows and writes at her home in the Pacific Northwest. She is the author of the children's book *Tub Toys* (Tricycle Press), written with her son, Tim Warner.

**Joyce Stark** ("Home Away from Home") lives in northeast Scotland, where she works part time for the local county government. Her dream is to write nonstop for nine months a year and to travel in the United States and Europe for the remaining three.

**Kelly L. Stone** ("Leaping Year Sisters"), a licensed mental health counselor and writer, hails from Atlanta, Georgia. She has published stories in magazines and in anthologies, including *A Cup of Comfort for Mothers & Daughters* and *A Cup of Comfort for Inspiration.*

**Shelley Ann Wake** ("Hair Care" and "Nudges and Lollies") spends most of her time writing essays, poems, stories, and children's books. Her work has been published in various magazines, e-zines, and anthologies in Australia, Great Britain, Canada, and the United States. She lives in Hunter Valley, Australia, with her husband, Tony.

**Joan Watt** ("The Green Coat"), a retiree, has been freelance writing for many years. Her work has appeared in *Guideposts, Indianapolis Star, Franklin Journal, Indianapolis*

*Monthly* magazine, and many other publications. She lives on a farm in Indiana, where she enjoys writing, reading, dabbling in watercolor painting, and her family.

**Amy Williams** ("Breathe") is a writer, wife, and mother to three children, who, she swears, are only on loan from another, more magical world. She lives in Northern Arizona, where she divides her time between writing, civic endeavors, and managing her family-owned business.

**Linda C. Wisniewski** ("Little Black Cat") has worked as a librarian, newspaper reporter, and freelance writer. She lives with her family in southeastern Pennsylvania and teaches memoir writing at Bucks County Community College. She enjoys reading mystery novels, practicing yoga, and watching her retired scientist husband cook fabulous gourmet meals.

**Audrey Yanes** ("Sisters of the San Joaquin") is a retired kindergarten teacher and the mother of nine off-spring. She has stood on the Great Wall in China, studied in the Galápagos, sailed the islands of Greece, and prayed at the Wailing Wall in Jerusalem. When not working on her memoirs, she enjoys rafting and writing poetry.

# About the Editor

Colleen Sell has long believed in the power of story to inspire and enrich our lives. Storytelling is both her passion and profession, and with it, she has fed her family and her soul for more than twenty-five years.

A freelance writer and editor, Colleen has published hundreds of articles and numerous books, including *10-Minute Zen* and eleven volumes of the Cup of Comfort book series. She is the former editor in chief of the award-winning *Biblio* and *Mercator's World* magazines, and has been a journalist, columnist, and copywriter.

She lives with her husband and border collie mutt on a lavender farm in the Pacific Northwest, where her sisters are among their most welcome guests.